Developed at warp-speed and designed for overwhelming victory, the Desert Storm air campaign lit up the skies of Baghdad and changed strategic thinking forever. Now, John Warden—architect of the Desert Storm air campaign—and his partner, organizational consultant Leland Russell, have applied this proven approach to success to another kind of intense competition: the fast-changing world of 21st century business.

The system—Prometheus—is a mindset and a method for rapid, decisive strategic action. Its essence is simple: think strategically, focus sharply and move quickly. Leaders and managers of big cap, mid-cap and startup companies, in high-tech finance, health care, and many other industries, have successfully applied Prometheus to meet the same kinds of challenges that you face.

Now, through clear, step-by-step directions and dramatic, behind-the-scenes stories, *Winning in FastTime* will explain Prometheus to you. Whether you are a CEO, a manager, a project leader, or simply a dedicated employee, this book will help you:

• Transform your organization into a nimble, market-leading winner;
• Design a Grand Strategy that everyone from the boardroom to the front line can share;
• Shape tomorrow ... before it shapes you.

Winning in FastTime has a powerful message. You can control your destiny ... if you are willing to shed yesterday's thinking about business strategy and organization... move fast and decisively ... and make the future what you want it to be. Welcome to the world of Prometheus.

Winning in *FastTime*

ALSO BY JOHN WARDEN

The Air Campaign: Planning for Combat

WINNING IN
Fast
TIME

Harness the
Competitive Advantage
of **Prometheus**
in Business and Life

John A. Warden III
Leland A. Russell

GEO Group Press books may be purchased for educational, business, or sales promotional use. For information address GEO Group Press, 4750 Von Karman, Newport Beach, CA 92660.

ISBN 0-9712697-0-X   paperback
ISBN 0-9712697-1-8   hardcover

Cover design by Paulette Livers, Livers Lambert Design,
    and Rita Swanson, GrafixWest
Book design by Nancy Singer Olaguera
Illustrations by Deborah Flora

10 9 8 7 6 5

To Margie, Betsy, and Johnny
and to Melissa and Simon

Contents

Preface: Hyper-Change   ix

Prometheus Touchstones

1. The Prometheus Process   3

2. Instant Thunder   9

3. Changing the Game   20

4. Centers of Gravity   32

Design the Future

5. The Environment   51

6. The Future Picture   63

7. Guiding Precepts   77

8. Measures of Merit   90

Target for Success

9. The Five Rings   109

10. Desired Effects   127

Campaign to Win

11. Parallel Campaigns   141

12. Organizing for Success   152

Finish with Finesse

13.   The Endgame   167

14.   Cardinal Rules   179

15.   Prometheus @ Work   191

Bibliography   199

Acknowledgments   205

Index   219

Preface: Hyper-Change

It may surprise you to learn that you witnessed the birth of a powerful business process—Prometheus—on global television. It was the evening of January 16, 1991, when the launch of the first hyper-war was broadcast live on CNN.

The incendiary display that marked the beginning of the Desert Storm air campaign, a time-compressed convergence of technology and strategy, made the world eyewitness to an event as fundamental as the Stone Age becoming the Bronze Age or the Council of Nicea marking the end of the Ancient Age and the beginning of the Medieval. Desert Storm marked the beginning of the age of hyper-change.

Now the era of warp-speed competition has arrived in business, and leaders everywhere are grappling with the extraordinary implications. How is it possible to plan strategically in an environment that can change in the twinkling of an electronic eye? How do you win in a warp-speed world?

The approach we offer—the Prometheus Process—is a mind-set and a method for rapid, decisive strategic action. No one could have expected that the fiery tempest of the Desert Storm air campaign would launch a new solution for doing business in the hyper-speed age. But the planning of that campaign became the benchmark for *Winning in FastTime*.

PROMETHEUS TOUCHSTONES

1

The Prometheus Process

"New circumstances require new approaches."

Prometheus—a name shrouded in mystery and antiquity. Why should a radically new approach to business success be called the *Prometheus Process?* The answer is easy. Prometheus, the wisest of the Titans in Greek mythology, is the ideal metaphor and beacon for winning in *FastTime:* forethought and fire.

The old Greek gods, according to the ancient myth, assigned to two brothers the responsibility of putting life on earth—Epimetheus, whose name means "hindsight," and Prometheus, whose name means "forethought." Epimetheus went first and populated the earth with all the animals. Then it fell to Prometheus to create man.

Prometheus saw that his brother had given the animals powerful survival tools: claws, speed, height, weight, and other physical attributes. He asked himself, "What is left for mankind?" Prometheus realized that man could prevail against stronger, faster adversaries only if he could outthink them; thus his first gift to mankind was forethought, the capacity to think ahead. Later, he realized that forethought alone was insufficient; man needed something else. The something else was fire—a source of energy and light so important that the gods kept it for themselves. Prometheus went to Mount Olympus, the home of Zeus and the other gods. From their very throne, he stole the fire of the gods and gave it to man. With forethought and fire, man could now overcome every obstacle—and he alone of the inhabitants of the earth had the power to create the future.

Today, forethought and fire (passion) fuel high-performing organizations. Those whose leaders think strategically and execute passionately have the ultimate competitive advantage—the power to spark their own success, illuminate the future, and ignite the energy of all of their stakeholders.

Create the future rather than fear it . . . this is the spirit of Prometheus.

A NEW WORLD

We live in an opportunity-rich world. Breakthroughs in health science, information technology, materials, marketing, consumer products, investments, transportation, energy—the whole range of human endeavors—are not only accelerating; they have also created a cornucopia of possibilities for new products, services, and business models.

But opportunity is only half the story. The fast-forward pace of technology, the rapid blurring of competitive boundaries, and the instantaneous mobility of capital spawn new challenges. Competitive threats and opportunities are no longer predictable in time, place, or specifics. Disruptive innovations, appearing at increasing speeds, can suddenly endanger an enterprise or an entire industry.

In today's radically different, mercurial marketplace, what does it take to win? A new model for strategic thinking and action is essential, a model designed for a world that operates on Internet Time. Traditional approaches are no longer adequate because, more often than not, they fail to keep pace with rapidly evolving marketplaces and ever-changing competitive scenarios.

A NEW WAY OF RUNNING AN ENTERPRISE

This book introduces the Prometheus Process— a new way of running an enterprise in a warp-speed world.

Prometheus is based on a fundamental assumption. You won't win in the twenty-first century by merely reacting to change, or making incremental improvements to maintain your current position. To win, you must decide what you want your tomorrow to be, and then make it happen faster than the rate of change in your competitive environment. This is winning in *FastTime.*

Prometheus is a systematic and proven method for designing winning strategies. The process itself is straightforward enough to grasp readily, yet sophisticated enough to use for planning, executing, and successfully completing projects of any scope and complexity. It guides you to focus on the future and to decide what the real measurements of success need to be; it teaches you how to find the right "targets" for action that will give you the most return on your energy; it shows you how to think about different organizational concepts; and it leads you to plan as carefully for the end of product and business cycles as for the beginnings.

Prometheus includes a common strategic vocabulary that is shared across the organization. When everyone from the boardroom to the front line is thinking strategically and using the same terminology, the effect is like a nuclear chain reaction. The human energy and results expand exponentially.

Prometheus is also *fractal*. This means that the same process pattern can be repeated over and over at an ever-smaller scale. Each division, department, and unit can use Prometheus to produce its own strategic plan, a plan that is linked and aligned with the Grand Strategy of the organization as a whole.

Why is it necessary for the whole organization to engage in strategy? The traditional approach, in which people are expected to embrace and execute a strategic plan developed in isolation by a senior executive team—or worse yet, by an outside consulting firm—is roughly akin to a football team on which only the quarterback knows the plays. Experience shows that people won't embrace something they don't fully understand, especially if they feel no sense of ownership.

On the other hand, if we engage people in the design of strategy, they will, at a minimum, grasp the intent of the strategy and therefore do a better job of executing it.

No plan is perfect, so we not only want people engaged in designing the plans they must execute, we also want them empowered as they move forward to make the many rapid, smart adjustment decisions that will inevitably be required. Empowered decision-making means that the decision-makers (and, in reality, that's almost everyone) must understand the Big Picture—the overall strategy.

To engage the whole organization in creating and executing winning plans, you need a *common framework* for strategic thinking. The Prometheus Process provides that framework. Once Prometheus is accepted and incorporated by the organization, everyone can move forward together in *FastTime*.

Most importantly, people will no longer be thinking like bricklayers. Bricklayers are specialists but are usually not concerned about the larger issues, such as how the community should be organized or what the purpose of the buildings should be. They are primarily concerned about the *details* of construction: How many bricks will we need? How high should this wall be?

The Prometheus Process helps people think like an architect rather than a bricklayer. It engages as many people as possible in the process of answering four strategic questions.

- What future do we want to create?
- What system change is necessary for that future to become reality?
- Which leverage points in the system will move it in the desired direction?
- How will we know when we're finished, and what is the exit plan?

When these questions are answered for the overall organization, the result is an overarching Grand Strategy. The process then becomes fractal—the same kinds of questions are answered at ever-lower levels until every unit of the organization has its own sub-strategy. This fractal approach builds a deep level of understanding, commitment, and alignment.

Over time, we've found that using the Prometheus Process leads to a new strategic mind-set in an organization. The day-to-day dialogue is no longer confined to tactical details, but begins to encompass larger, longer-term issues. Groups within the organization find new ways to connect to one another. People who, on the surface, appear to have little in common, begin to work together like teams of architects planning a new community.

These ideas, if followed carefully, will substantially improve your probability of success in business whether you are an individual, a sole proprietor, a manager, or the chairman of a global enterprise.

ABOUT THIS BOOK

In the pages that follow we explain the powerful business process we have successfully introduced to corporate clients across the United States. We show you a new way to run your enterprise, an approach that fits the realities of the twenty-first century.

Prometheus is the result of a creative collaboration between John Warden, the man behind the historic, winning Desert Storm air campaign, and Leland Russell, the creator of the *GEO Paradigm,* a model designed to enable organizations to succeed in an era of complex, unpredictable, rapid change. The first time we met we discovered that we had something in common: a passion for helping our clients create the future. In 1999 we formed Prometheus Strategies, Inc., which merges our proven, breakthrough approaches.

Chorus:	Did you go further than you have told us?
Prometheus:	I caused mortals to cease foreseeing doom.

From Prometheus Bound *by Aeschylus*
Translation by Seth G. Benardete

Chapter Debrief: the Prometheus Process

In today's warp-speed world, a new approach that accelerates strategic thinking and action is essential.

To win, you must decide what you want your tomorrow to be, and then make it happen faster than the rate of change in your competitive environment. This is winning in *FastTime.*

The Prometheus Process is a systematic and proven method for designing winning strategies that is simple enough for everyone to grasp, yet sophisticated enough to use in planning, executing, and completing projects of any scope and complexity.

Prometheus includes a common strategic vocabulary that is shared across the organization. It is also *fractal,* which means that the same process pattern can be repeated over and over on an ever-smaller scale.

2

Instant Thunder

"Think strategically, focus sharply, and move quickly."

What does it take to win in a world where change is not only rapid but accelerating, where ancient "truths" collapse with disconcerting regularity, where fortunes are made and lost in hours and months rather than in decades?

The basic formula for winning in the twenty-first century is simple: think strategically, focus sharply, and move quickly. We've labeled this Instant Thunder and it's one of the cornerstones of Prometheus.

The term "Instant Thunder" comes from the code name for the air campaign in the first hyper-war—Desert Storm. Because this was a rapid, decisive victory that harnessed revolutionary concepts about strategy, it contains valuable lessons for another battlefield: the fast-changing world of twenty-first-century business.

INSTANT THUNDER: THE CHALLENGE

When Iraqi forces poured over the border and overran neighboring Kuwait in 1990, General Norman Schwarzkopf faced the same kind of challenge that corporate managers and leaders frequently find themselves facing these days: A drastic, unexpected change has occurred and a new plan of action is needed *now*.

Normally military plans require months, even years, to develop. Yet the Instant Thunder plan was developed from scratch in just forty-eight hours, and would be the decisive factor in winning the Gulf War.

How had it been possible to create a winning plan in only two days? And what benefits does that process—Prometheus—hold for business?

In retrospect, it's easy to forget that this victory (and the speed of it) was not expected. There were serious concerns, not only about the potential for political fallout around the world, but also about whether it was possible to defeat Iraq militarily, given the disappointments in Korea and Vietnam.

There was good reason for such concerns. In July of 1990, Saddam Hussein was one of the most powerful men in the world. Washington and Moscow courted him, Riyadh feared him, and the price of oil responded instantly to his veiled threats and feints. What's more, he had the fourth biggest conventional (non-nuclear) military machine in the world, with a capability that eclipsed that of yesterday's Great Powers like Britain, Germany, and France. Not only was the raw military power there, but also the experience of using it brutally and effectively—and the willingness to do so again.

On the morning of Thursday, August 2, 1990, residents of Kuwait City looked out of their windows and were horrified when they saw something they knew could never be—Iraqi tanks in their streets, appearing out of nowhere, without warning. Saddam Hussein had executed a brilliant and logistically challenging *coup de main*. He now owned Kuwait. The price of oil in the world market began a rapid upward spiral. It would double within sixty days.

At the time of the invasion, John Warden, coauthor of this book, was on a cruise with his family, taking a long-delayed vacation from his duties as the officer responsible for developing United States Air Force strategy, doctrine, and long-range plans.

On shipboard television, John saw Iraqi tanks rolling through Kuwait. For years he had been thinking about how to deal with such a crisis, and now found himself trapped on a cruise liner south of Cuba. John recalls the experience:

> There was no way to get off the ship, so I was stuck there for a day and a half while it slowly made its way back to Miami. But during those thirty-six hours, I realized that the existing war plans assumed we were playing defense. Worse, at least within the planning staffs, I knew there was no real grasp of offensive strategy.

The problem was perspective. All prior planning, literally thousands of hours, had been focused on the defense of Saudi Arabia against a large aggressor force. But the Kuwait situation didn't fit these plans at all because it was not a defensive problem. It was an offensive problem. The Iraqis now owned Kuwait and they were already in position to keep it forever.

With no way to escape what had now become a prison for him, John could only wait during the agonizingly slow return to the port of Miami . . . wait, and think about what could be done to reverse the Iraqi attack. He suspected (rightly, as it turned out) that all the major military and civilian staffs in Washington and in military headquarters around the world would be unlikely to propose an offensive strategy.

On Sunday morning, finally back in Washington, John confirmed his fears about the advice being proffered to President Bush and the National Security Council. So the following morning he assembled a small team to begin thinking about constructing and "selling" an offensive, game-changing plan.

Fortunately, General Norman Schwarzkopf, the brilliant commander of Central Command—the organization that had responsibility for the Middle East and Persian Gulf areas—did not need to be sold. He had already come to the same conclusion: Offensive action was necessary, and would need to start quickly.

Schwarzkopf was not only a brilliant military commander and leader, he was also a man who cared little for traditional approaches. Exasperated by the recommendations pouring in from Washington and from his own people, he took the unusual step of calling the Air Force Chief of Staff to see if he had any better ideas.

From the Vice Chief, General "Mike" Loh, General Schwarzkopf learned there was a group looking at exactly that idea. Schwarzkopf was delighted to hear this, but more than mildly skeptical about Loh's promise that this team would be able to give him a comprehensive plan on Friday morning, less than forty-eight hours away.

When the conversation with Schwarzkopf ended, Loh immediately called John Warden.

INSTANT THUNDER: PLANNING TO WIN

Just two hours after meeting with General Loh and receiving Schwarzkopf's request, John assembled in the basement of the Pentagon a large group drawn from across the staff and began a *FastTime* planning process. He fashioned for the group a high-level goal: to develop an executable plan focused on creating a better postwar situation for the United States and her friends in the Middle East.

At the heart of the plan would be an all-out offensive air campaign against Iraq. The plan was code-named "Instant Thunder," a deliberate contrast to the disastrous, graduated response of the "Rolling Thunder" plan that had been unsuccessful in Vietnam. This time around, there would be nothing gradual.

The planning group faced a daunting task: War plans typically take years to develop, but there were less than two days to come up with something that would work in the real world, where political considerations frequently override military logic. It was clear that neither the plan nor the planning process could be traditional in any way.

By Thursday, the group had grown to over two hundred people and had taken over the large briefing room of one of the Air Staff planning divisions, known as "Checkmate." This room, which was undivided by any doors or even cubicle walls, was the ideal environment for what we call "Open Planning."

On August 10, 1990—less than forty-eight hours after receiving the mandate—John and a few of his associates flew to General Schwarzkopf's headquarters at MacDill AFB near Tampa, where he presented a strategic, offensive air plan to General Schwarzkopf and his two key generals. Schwarzkopf listened carefully to the thirty-minute presentation, then responded enthusiastically. "You are the first guys that have been leaning forward," he said. "This is exactly what I want."

The general was ready to move, promising to place an immediate call to General Colin Powell, the Chairman of the Joint Chiefs of Staff. "I'll tell him I like this plan, that I want him to hear your presentation as soon as you get back to Washington, and that I want his support."

Sixteen hours later John was briefing General Powell. At the end of the presentation Powell pushed his chair back from the table and said, "Good plan. Very fine piece of work."

Just three days had elapsed since General Schwarzkopf's call to General Loh—but in that time, John and his planning group had developed, presented, and won approval for an air campaign to reverse Saddam Hussein's fortunes.

Within a week of the initial approval, General Schwarzkopf had an expanded, more detailed version of Instant Thunder, and John was on his way to Riyadh to deliver the plan to Lieutenant General Chuck Horner, the officer who would be responsible for its execution.

By mid-January, all elements were in place. On January 16, 1991, at 7 P.M. Washington time, the world watched—live on CNN—as the first hyper-war began.

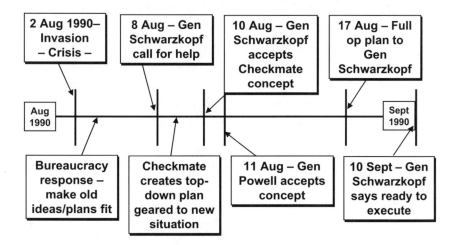

Figure 2.1 Large-Scale Integrated Planning—The Gulf War Air Campaign

INSTANT THUNDER: FAST, PRECISE, PARALLEL OPERATIONS

At the core of the Instant Thunder plan were smartly conceived, high-velocity operations designed to maximize results and minimize risk. Because of the speed and precision with which these operations were unleashed, the impact on Iraq was instantaneous and catastrophic.

During the *first twenty-four hours alone,* the air campaign attacked almost 150 Iraqi "Center of Gravity" targets carefully selected to create a devastating systemwide impact on Iraq. This was a thousand-fold time compression of the aerial bombardment the Germans had survived in 1943. Within minutes, Iraq's high command was left virtually blind, deaf, and dumb. Its leaders couldn't see what was coming at them; they could not assess the damage, and had no way to marshal resources to effect repairs or responses.

Attacked with unprecedented precision, Iraq's leadership facilities, command centers, national communications, electrical systems, air defense headquarters, and crucial biological and nuclear warfare centers ceased to function at a useful level. These fast, precise, parallel attacks, followed by a hundred-hour ground campaign, paralyzed Iraq and drove Saddam Hussein to sue for peace. Forty-one days after the initiation of hostilities, Iraq withdrew from Kuwait and accepted peace terms that stripped it of the regional superpower status it had previously enjoyed. Moreover, Iraq ceased being a strategic threat to its neighbors—a circumstance that, a decade later, still prevails.

In the Gulf War a sudden unexpected challenge was successfully addressed, rapidly and decisively. The revolutionary strategy and planning concepts harnessed to accomplish this are key to the Prometheus Process. Among the concepts you will find developed in subsequent chapters are the following:

Use an "Open Planning" Approach

Because the planning of the air war was a massive, complex undertaking that had to be compressed into a very short time period,

John Warden brought together people with as many different perspectives as possible, to think and plan openly with each other in the same workspace. This was the antithesis of most military planning efforts in which participation is limited to a select few.

In an environment of intense global competition defined by blinding speed and information overload, business leaders—regardless of how smart they are—don't have all of the answers. Open Planning leads to better decisions because there is a broader base of expertise and knowledge available. In addition, there's a greater likelihood that the plan will be successfully executed because a larger number of people understand the nuances and have a sense of ownership.

Decide What Future You Intend to Create

The planners' first step in Desert Storm was to define the strategic objectives. One was the future they wanted to create: a more stable Middle East, without open war, and where oil was flowing and people were doing business peacefully. They also described how strategic success would be measured: 1) Iraq has withdrawn from Kuwait; 2) Kuwaiti sovereignty has been restored; 3) the free flow of oil has been secured.

This "design the future" approach to strategic planning is essential in today's fast, complex business environment. Analyzing reams of information and then extrapolating your way up to a strategy is simply not practical. It takes too long and the plan that emerges is too tenuous. The place to begin is with the high-level *outcomes*. In Prometheus parlance, this is called your Future Picture. Once you are clear about the desired high-level results, then you can move down level by level into the details.

Know What You're Willing to Do or Not Do

The plan for the Desert Storm air campaign included "Guiding Precepts" to ensure that the war was against Saddam and his policies (not the Iraqi people), that civilian loss of life be kept to an absolute minimum; and that the war be fought in a way that capitalized on American strengths while avoiding entanglement where Iraq was dangerously capable.

Clearly articulating behavioral expectations is also important in business. Be clear about what kind of behavior you expect in your organization, as well as the ideals and style that are important to you. Address these issues early on in your strategic planning process, because this may affect your strategic choices.

Measure Strategically

In the Vietnam War, progress was measured by how many bombs had been dropped and how many of the enemy had been killed. These measures were not strategic in any sense. They measured the quantity and quality of tactics, but such statistics did not help to answer the important strategic question: Are we closer or further away from winning the war?

That error did not occur in Desert Storm. There were explicit measures to determine the *strategic* progress of the air campaign. These strategic measures did not address typical tactical concerns, like the number of targets hit or the number of bombs dropped. Those statistics were simply not relevant to strategic success. The planners were concerned only with the *effect* of the attacks on the enemy; in other words, they were interested in the overall results—how the campaign impacted on the functionality of the enemy "system" and how it was contributing to the achievement of postwar objectives.

In the business world, company after company measures the quality and quantity of its tactical actions—the number of sales calls, speed of delivery, or total minutes of network advertising. But you could double your sales calls, halve the delivery times, or quadruple advertising minutes, think you were doing great, and yet see your quarterly profits plunge and your stock price go with it. Without strategic measures—measures that connect your actions with the increased value you're trying to create—you're almost certain to make the same kinds of errors that military commanders regularly made before Desert Storm.

Change the System

The planners of Desert Storm had a systems perspective. Focusing on Iraq as an overall system, they saw that if they could drive the nation-state into a condition of paralysis, its tactical arm—its military forces—would lose their potency and Saddam would have no choice but to acquiesce to the demands of the coalition.

In business your global market, your industry, your competitors, even your own organization, all form a system. Companies that succeed don't design strategies for a single goal. They design strategies that transform the very system in which they operate. They re-create their environment in order to create their success.

Focus on Centers of Gravity

It may surprise you to learn that resources were an issue in Desert Storm. In order to leverage the resources that were available to the best strategic advantage, air operations concentrated on the "Centers of Gravity" in Iraq—leverage points in the system—where the resources used would have the greatest impact.

Every business, regardless of its size, wants to spend fewer resources rather than more in doing the job at hand. How do you use limited resources to best advantage? Target the available resources against the Centers of Gravity that exist in every market and every organization. Those leverage points could be specific customers, processes, facilities, or other key factors that allow you to produce a much higher return on committed resources than any other options.

Attack in Parallel

Why do we call Desert Storm the first hyper-war? It used air power to attack—in parallel—multiple Centers of Gravity *simultaneously*.

This parallel approach had an instant and catastrophic effect on the nation-state of Iraq.

The parallel approach can also achieve rapid change in an organization or a marketplace. Why? Both are systems and systems resist change—but systems can't resist when you go after many key leverage points at the same time.

Know When and How to Get Out

Every war ends, as do all companies, products, and services. The tendency in both war and business, however, is to avoid planning for the inevitable finish.

A critical part of Desert Storm planning was how to get out. Since the war, some people have criticized the decision of not going to Baghdad and "finishing the job." The critics make an essential point: Failure to end an enterprise well can wipe out the gains that have been made. A key measure is whether your real objectives have been reached.

In the Gulf, when the allies accepted Iraq's agreement to their peace terms, Desert Storm had in fact achieved its high-level objectives: Iraq was out of Kuwait, the Kuwaiti government was in the process of being restored, regional stability was palpably higher, and there was a resumption of normal commerce in the region. Iraq, per plan, appeared to be unable to threaten its neighbors strategically for at least a decade. All this had taken place in less than six weeks of war—and the cost had been historically low. In contrast, had the President agreed to "mission creep," the cost of the war would have soared, the coalition partners would have split, and the United States would have been doomed to occupy Iraq for years.

Desert Storm was a coalition effort with a complex political structure. In light of the strategic objectives and the costs that would have been incurred to change those objectives, the war was a resounding success. Leaders of business enterprises typically have much greater freedom of movement than political leaders. Yet all too many still fail to factor a successful finish into their goals.

Most executives and product managers excuse the lack of termination planning by saying that they cannot plan for the end until they know what the end is going to be, or by claiming that such planning would create a self-fulfilling prophecy. But if we know that everything is going to end, then we are irresponsible if we don't plan to make that end as good as possible, and to give us the best possible base for the next competition.

A GAME-CHANGING PLAN

To achieve the "Instant Thunder" effect—rapid victory at minimal cost—each one of these steps in the Prometheus Process plays a role. Taken together, they lead to a game-changing plan—a plan that carries you from concept to execution.

Chapter Debrief: Instant Thunder

The basic formula for winning in the twenty-first century is simple: Think strategically, focus sharply, and move quickly.

Instant Thunder was also the code name for the first hyper-war— the Desert Storm air campaign. At the core of this campaign were smartly conceived, high-velocity operations designed to maximize results and minimize risk.

The revolutionary strategy and planning concepts harnessed in Desert Storm are the foundation of the Prometheus Process:

- Use an "Open Planning" approach.
- Decide what future you intend to create.
- Know what you're willing to do and not do.
- Measure strategically.
- Change the system.
- Focus on Centers of Gravity.
- Attack in parallel.
- Know when and how to get out.

3

Changing the Game

"When you make the rules, it is easy to win the game."

In the intense, high-velocity environment of twenty-first-century business, one thing is certain. You won't win by following the rules of yesterday.

Think about it: In almost every industry today there are two kinds of organizations. First, there are those like Microsoft, Charles Schwab, MCI WorldCom, and Dell that change the game; they shape the rules to their advantage. All the other organizations in those industries are left to follow in their footsteps. When the competitive rules change, the followers must do the best they can to adapt. The game-changers have a significant advantage because, since they are creating the future, they understand the future better than their competitors do. Since they leave the starting gate before their competition, the game-changers get first crack at mind share and market share. Wall Street loves them because they build new markets and new wealth for investors.

What does it take to be the kind of game-changing organization that the Prometheus Process envisions? At the very highest level, a determination to create the future requires having a Grand Strategy, an encompassing, integrated plan that will take the organization from idea to execution to completion. Absent a Grand Strategy, an organization is at the mercy of unpredictable, random events.

A Grand Strategy is a fundamental of the Prometheus Process; at the heart of a Grand Strategy must be a well-grounded understanding of what "strategy" truly is and what it isn't.

STRATEGY—A SUPERIOR APPROACH

Game-changing organizations may or may not have the deepest pockets, or the latest and greatest tools, or even the most qualified and educated people. But invariably they have one thing in common—a superior strategic approach to their competitive challenges.

It was a superior strategy that won the 1991 Persian Gulf War. Iraq's *coup de main* the previous August—suddenly attacking Kuwait and digging in—could easily have succeeded. Military experts in Washington concluded that even in the best-case scenario it would be difficult, if not impossible, for liberating forces to invade Kuwait without destroying the country in the process. The loss of life would have been horrendous: According to one report in the *Washington Post* shortly after the Iraqi invasion, the Pentagon estimated that over 20,000 Americans would have died in a direct assault on Kuwait.

If General Schwarzkopf had proposed a *mano a mano* solution to President Bush, with its accompanying high casualty rates, it is highly unlikely that the President would have been able to secure the political support for a war with Iraq. Under these circumstances, there would have been no Gulf War, Saddam would still be in Kuwait, and the world would be markedly different.

Desert Storm succeeded because it changed the game on Saddam Hussein. By capitalizing on American strengths—not only superior technology but a systematic "Centers of Gravity" targeting approach—this strategy achieved success far faster, with far fewer casualties, than anyone except its architects expected.

Similarly, Dell changed the computer hardware game with a brilliant new business model that left tactically focused rivals like Compaq in the dust. "Direct from Dell" leveraged the capabilities of the Internet to create a virtual organization that not only eliminated the middleman, but also rewrote the rules of inventory management and product distribution: In the meantime, competitors were continually improving by making marginal changes to their equipment and their existing distribution systems. Strategy trumps tactics.

Can a mom-and-pop retail operation think and act strategically? An Internet start-up? A manufacturing plant? A not-for-profit charity? Not only is the answer yes, but failure to think and act strategically at every level and every size of business is a prescription for failure in a world where your tactics can be copied in a moment. Strategies, on the other hand, are much harder to copy.

TACTICS VERSUS STRATEGY

What are the fundamental distinctions between strategy and tactics? Even many of the most astute business people frequently confuse the two.

Tactics are day-to-day activities that are repeatable and relatively unambiguous. Like blocking and tackling in football, they comprise the basic components of the jobs in an organization— making a sales call on a client, operating a machine on an assembly line, sending out bills in an accounting department. But the list goes on to include broader, less obvious activities as well, such as cutting costs or selling over the Internet—quick fixes that can bring short-term gains, but often lead to changes that erode these gains.

No question, tactical excellence is important. But will superior tactics alone ensure long-term success? In other words, if we are better than our competitors in how we do our day-to-day jobs and how we struggle within the current competitive game, will we win over time?

Probably not. It's bad enough that your competitors can copy your tactics so easily, but while you're focused on tactics, sooner or later someone will come along and change the game with a better strategy. Superior tactics can't protect you from that.

Many people assume that doing *more* of a tactical activity or doing it *better* is a strategy: "Our strategy is to increase the number of sales calls per month." But scaling up the quantity of tactics or improving the quality of tactics is rarely a strategy—and it almost never delivers the desired outcome.

In April 2000, Wall Street woke up to the fact that the "strategy" of many of the dot.com retailers—direct selling over the Internet— was simply a tactic. Once the traditional retailers grasped the implications of what was happening in the new e-economy, they were easily able to duplicate the "sell over the Net" tactic pioneered by the dot.coms. Many of the brick-and-mortar retailers, like Barnes & Noble, quickly became *click*-and mortar retailers. Almost everyone failed to make money because too many organizations were offering the same low-margin services. In this tactical environment, survival meant price competition, which rapidly commoditized the business area and squeezed margins. As investors saw what was happening, they dumped their dot.com positions and drove the price of dot.com stocks to a fraction of their previous levels.

THE 38TH-PARALLEL PHENOMENON

Mistaking tactics for strategy sets you up for the back-and-forth tactical competition we call the "38th-Parallel Phenomenon." The name is a reference to the Korean War.

In June of 1950, the North Koreans launched a surprise attack on South Korea. It was a very strategic move and it certainly "changed the game"—the status quo—on the Korean peninsula. Soon the North Koreans had succeeded in driving the South Koreans and a handful of Americans all the way down the peninsula, conquering almost all of the South. (Strategic Move 1 in Figure 3.1)

The commander of the U.S. and United Nations forces, General Douglas MacArthur, countered with a bold, game-changing strategy of his own: a daring amphibious landing at Inchon, well behind

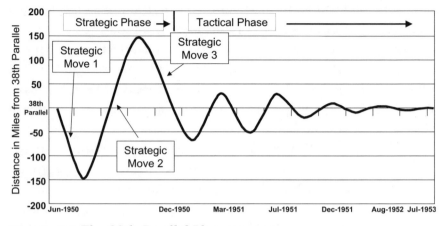

Figure 3.1 The 38th-Parallel Phenomenon

the North Korean lines. It succeeded brilliantly: In a very short time, MacArthur moved all the way up the peninsula and conquered North Korea. (Move 2, Figure 3.1)

Now the Chinese, unhappy about having Americans camped on the border of their country, decided to intervene. They launched their own surprise strategic offensive, attacking in large numbers in December 1950. The Chinese assault drove U.S. forces back to a point just below the center of the peninsula, at a latitude known as the 38th Parallel. (Move 3, Figure 3.1)

This was the last strategic move in the entire war. From this point on, the game did not change. It became a grueling and expensive tactical competition, with one side and then the other introducing more troops, more ammunition, or newer weapons. For the next two years the front moved back and forth across the 38th Parallel with neither side achieving sustained advantage. Sadly, it was during these two years that the majority of lives were lost.

Many companies, especially in mature markets, have long been locked in tactical competitions like the Korean War. For example, in 1957, TWA became the first airline to offer fresh-brewed coffee. When the competition matched the move, TWA four years later became the first to offer in-flight movies. Both attractive ideas, but both tactical. In time, almost all airlines on their longer flights had movies as well as fresh-brewed coffee. The movies, and other 38th-Parallel tactical offerings like frequent-flyer programs, are now costly extras that the airline CEOs probably wish they could dump. The computer memory-chip business is also a 38th-Parallel competition, based almost exclusively on pricing. One manufacturer figures out a way to reduce the production cost of the memory chip and then a competitor figures out a way to reduce it a bit more. Each time someone temporarily gains an advantage, but the end result is that no one makes sustained profits or gains a sustained competitive advantage.

In the quick-service restaurant industry, if sales are down for Burger King, the company typically responds with tactical moves—adding a new menu item, improving drive-through service, or lowering prices. Will throwing energy at these problems drive sales up again? In the short run, maybe. But what happens when McDonald's, Wendy's and others see the Burger King move? They lower their prices, too; add new menu items, too; pump up service, too. Everybody works harder but the businesses gain little from the effort and the investment—and may easily find themselves worse off than before they initiated the moves.

How do you know when you're locked in cyclical, tactical-level competition—battling back and forth across your own particular 38th Parallel? Everyone works harder and harder with fewer and fewer results. The sad truth is that it probably doesn't matter much how hard people work or how many refinements they make to the existing products and services. At some point, there are but two possibilities: The organization takes a new strategic path or, bypassed by competition, it begins drifting, losing ground, heading toward a downward spiral.

THE ADVANTAGES OF STRATEGY

Unlike good tactics, good strategies are difficult to duplicate. They change many things, quickly. They provide for *early* success, then set the stage for *sustained* success.

Strategies have a number of interrelated elements, and the best act upon a system as a whole. They might create a new market space (eBay); or offer a superior business model (Dell Computers); or become a dominant "portal" brand (Yahoo!). A good strategy may alter the competitive scenario in ways that may not be immediately obvious to outsiders. Many people wondered why Microsoft licensed its DOS operating system not just to IBM but to other companies as well. Microsoft knew why: By creating an industry-standard PC operating system, it could bypass the hardware business and dominate the computer industry from a totally new direction.

Herb Kelleher, who reinvented air travel when he founded Southwest Airlines, understood strategy. He knew that many airline passengers would eagerly forgo extras like in-flight meals, reserved seats, and the like in exchange for bargain fares. He also understood that elements like reliable, on-time service were considered essential, something many travelers would not give up just to get a lower fare. As co-founder and then as CEO, Kelleher built Southwest Airlines on these principles—a set of ideas that he brought together as had no one else. Under him the airline rapidly grew from a small, regional carrier to a force that has influenced the industry. His ideas were not tactical; in combination, they were quintessentially strategic.

Strategic moves are especially difficult for competitors to discern when they are indirect and long-term. For example, when the Japanese automakers moved to capture U.S. market share in the early sixties, they did not take on Detroit's Big Three directly. Detroit's focus was on the big cars everyone seemed to want—Chevy Impalas, Ford Fairlanes, Cadillacs, and the like. If the Japanese had gone after this big-car market, they would have run into significant opposition. A direct attack would have been answered directly. So, instead, the Japanese began by introducing tiny, cheap cars, the kind of cars Detroit believed no American would buy. The Japanese began a marketing campaign in California—far from the experts in Motor City. Detroit's Big Three paid scant attention to what the Japanese were doing and made no effort, for instance, to block imports with tariff legislation or to counter with their own small cars.

What did the Japanese accomplish with this indirect strategic approach? They began to build a reputation in the automobile market for quality and low price. Still flying under the radar screen, they quietly assembled a network of dealers around the United States. Slowly but surely, their market share grew: In 1962 it was 4 percent; by 1967 it had risen to 10 percent; by 1974 it was up to 15 percent; by the early 1980s it was 21 percent; and by the time the Big Three finally woke up around 1989, the Japanese had 30 percent of the market. For over a quarter of a century, Detroit suffered from the "Boiled-Frog Syndrome"—they just sat there unaware while the heat was slowly turned up.

A superior strategy will trump superior tactics. A classic example is the battle between Apple and IBM-compatible PCs. In the late 1970s Apple was one of the first to reach the market with what we now call personal computers. When the IBM-compatible PC was introduced in 1981, most people agreed that it was inferior to Apple's computers for several reasons. It was not as attractive or as ergonomically designed; it was far more difficult to use and had a less stable operating system. Yet the IBM-compatible PC captured 90 percent of the worldwide market in computers and set the standard for the industry.

What happened?

Apple had superior manufacturing and design tactics. But it lost the desktop war because the proponents of IBM-compatible PCs—which eventually included Dell, Compaq, Hewlett-Packard, and Gateway, to name a few—had a superior strategy for approaching the emerging desktop market.

The "compatible PC" strategy was based on an open architecture and permission to clone. With multiple hardware manufacturers all using similar technology, the PC paradigm quickly came to dominate the market. It was nimble, and quickly mutated to meet changing market conditions. This proved to be a superior approach to the competitive challenges of the emerging desktop market. It allowed the technically inferior PC to win the market because it changed the rules of the game, a game that Apple had initially created. Even superior tactics are not a guarantee of strategic success.

The lesson is clear: Victory flows from strategic merit, not tactical merit.

THE SINE QUA NON OF WINNING

A good strategy is the sine qua non, the necessary precondition, of winning. A superior approach, aggressively executed, enables organizations even with limited resources to accomplish the seemingly impossible.

Case in point: Who won the Vietnam War?

Most of us think that winning wars means winning the most important battles. In the long years of the Vietnam War, the United States won almost all the battles and imposed frightfully high losses on the Viet Cong and the North Vietnamese military. Despite all these successes, however, it was North Vietnam who raised her flag over Saigon in 1975, promptly renaming it Ho Chi Minh City.

How did the North Vietnamese accomplish this? North Vietnam's strategy took into account the fact that its forces were militarily inferior to the U.S. forces. While the United States thought the important war was in the jungles of Indochina, the North Vietnamese understood that the real war was the psychological one being fought in the heartland of America; they succeeded in affecting American public opinion despite losing battles and suffering terrible losses on the battlefield and from aerial attack. Their strategy trumped American tactical brilliance—and also demonstrated that there is a way to affect any large system when you understand its leverage points.

Whether it's on the battlefield or in the marketplace, you can prevail even when all conventional analysis would say that your resources are simply inadequate. It just takes superior strategy.

STRATEGY AND LEADERSHIP

Since a good Grand Strategy is the key to a sustainable competitive advantage, it's logical to assume that leaders in every organization would make this their top priority. Yet very few leaders spend more than cursory time in this critical area. In their book, *Competing for the Future,* Gary Hamel and C. K. Prahalad estimate that senior managers devote less than 3 percent of their time to building a corporate perspective on the future.

In fact, it shouldn't be surprising that long-term thinking is rare in most organizations. People are conditioned their whole lives to think tactically: Cross the street without paying attention or you get run over by a truck. Tackle the guy carrying the ball or your team loses the football game. Learn the assigned set of facts or you fail the test.

When we enter the world of business, we soon learn that the key to career success is completing the assigned job at hand. Prepare financials on time. Make the sales quotas. Most leaders never make the leap from tactical thinking to strategic thinking. They simply take the tactical lessons they've learned over a lifetime and apply them at the strategic level. Addressing the broad, long-term plan for an organization's success is often viewed as too theoretical. The practical leader rolls up the sleeves and does "real" work—making something happen now!

It's not easy to rise above short-term urgencies to focus on what's truly important for the long run. This is bad news for organizations in general, but offers a golden opportunity for those willing to think long-term. Focusing on creating the future with a winning strategy will pay huge dividends, whether you're running a small work group or a large enterprise.

Consider the case of our client Texas Instruments. For over ten years, the market capitalization of Texas Instruments (TI) was flat. This was during a period when many of its competitors, including Intel and Motorola, were experiencing substantial growth in their market capitalization. The performance of TI's stock was an indication that the investment community was not impressed with the company's prospects.

By the mid 1990s, many of the senior executives at Texas Instruments began to realize that the company's problem did not lie with its tactical capabilities. The company had invented the integrated circuit, had developed the signal-processing power that was the heart of the Gulf War's laser-guided bombs, and had won the coveted Malcolm Baldrige National Quality Award. The real problem, the executives believed, was inadequate strategy. Two of them, Tom Engibous and Rich Templeton (who would become Chairman and

CEO of Texas Instruments, and Executive Vice President and Chief Operating Officer of Texas Industries, respectively), led the charge to find and adopt new strategic approaches to their business.

Applying many of the principles presented in this book, TI refocused and started thinking strategically. It reevaluated all of its business units and decided to shed most of its businesses—including "sacred cows" like its cyclical memory chip, and profitable defense businesses that were no longer in alignment with its new strategic direction. Instead of fighting Intel and Samsung for a share of the chip market, or trying to be a portfolio company, TI targeted the explosive market for digital signal processors—DSPs—a key component of Internet and mobile communication devices. "DSPs," says Engibous, "are the engines of the digital age."

As *Forbes* magazine observed, TI's strategic moves were awfully smart in retrospect. Today the company dominates the DSP market—more than half of all cellular phones are equipped with TI's chips. As shown in Figure 3.2, TI's new strategy has also had a dramatic impact on its market capitalization, which within three years increased sixfold.

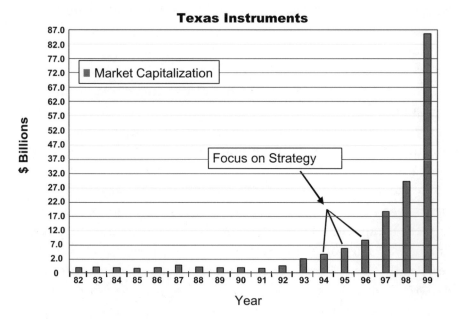

Figure 3.2 The Impact of Strategy

Remember, Texas Instruments' outstanding tactical abilities hadn't changed. Only its strategy.

Chapter Debrief: Changing the Game

Game-changing organizations understand the future better than others because they are creating it.

The common characteristic in game-changing organizations is a superior approach to their competitive challenges, a winning strategy.

A strategy is a blueprint that describes the future reality you want and provides a high-level road map for getting there. That blueprint is essential for building and sustaining success.

Unlike good tactics, good strategies are difficult to duplicate. They have a number of interrelated elements, acting upon a system as a whole, and they can alter the competitive scenario in ways that may not be immediately obvious to others.

4

Centers of Gravity

"To create the future you must transform the system."

Many consider the Desert Storm air campaign to be the benchmark for winning in *FastTime*. What was the secret to this phenomenal success? Was it more than speed? Better-trained personnel? Superior technology?

Those were certainly factors, but they do not account for the precision of the campaign or the magnitude of the victory. There was something more significant, more fundamental: a strategic-systems approach to strategy and a new perspective.

This was the real differentiator, the "magic" that led to the quick victory—and the element missed by most outsiders.

A Prometheus-designed strategy focuses on the true "enemy" of success, and that is not your competitors in the market or the advocates of the status quo within your organization. The true "enemy" is always the current system in which you operate as a whole. To create the future, you must change the system. How do you do that?

The Desert Storm air campaign is an excellent case study in the technique. It was based on a system strategy that was specifically designed to undermine the nation-state system of Iraq by precisely and rapidly striking key leverage points in the system—"Centers of Gravity" like communications centers, command centers, electrical facilities, and petroleum refineries. The collapse of Iraq as a system automatically put the Iraqi army in Kuwait in a hopeless position, where it would eventually starve or go home.

You may be thinking, "Sure, it worked in a military campaign, but that's not the same thing as business."

Since 1995, we have guided numerous organizations, small and large, in applying the system approach to strategy, in a variety of industries including high-tech, entertainment, finance, health care, construction, Internet start-ups, and food service.

Why does this systems approach proven in Desert Storm work equally well in business? The answer has to do with what we mean by a system.

THE NATURE OF SYSTEMS

Every business action or tactic must be executed within a system. A product-marketing approach happens within a market—which is a system. An internal-change attempt takes place within the context of an organization—which is a system. Failure to recognize that actions take place within a system means that your efforts will affect only one part of the whole, while the rest resists vigorously. By focusing your efforts against the entire system to achieve rapid system change, you increase your probability of success significantly.

Creating winning system strategies requires an understanding of the nature of systems. All systems have two essential characteristics. First, the whole accomplishes something that none of the parts can do alone. For example, what is the function of the mechanical system we call an automobile? Its function is to transport you from one place to another. No single part of an automobile can do that alone.

The second characteristic shared by all systems is that the performance of the whole and that of the parts are interdependent. If your new Mercedes gets a flat tire, the whole car is stuck. The entire system's function of transporting you is affected.

These two ideas emerged in academic circles during the 1940s and were popularized during the 1990s by MIT professor Peter Senge. In his best-seller *The Fifth Discipline,* Senge defined "systems thinking" as:

- Seeing interrelationships rather than linear cause-effect chains.
- Seeing processes of change over time rather than as static snap-shots.

Despite its relevance to strategy, systems thinking has not been widely embraced in leadership and planning circles. "Our leaders' eyes glaze over when you bring up the subject of systems thinking," says John Baum, former Director of Executive Education for Texas Instruments. "They've seen no evidence that systems thinking can be used to solve their problems."

The Gulf air war planners did not approach systems in an academic way; rather they focused on how to achieve rapid, real-world system change. The approach was hard-nosed and action-oriented: "What do we want Iraq as a system to look like after this campaign? What system change is necessary to get there?"

THE SISYPHUS SYNDROME

System change is no mean feat because all dynamic systems are "hardwired" to resist change vigorously.

Recall the story of Sisyphus, condemned by the Greek gods to push a boulder up a hill: As soon as he reached the top and thought he had succeeded, the boulder rolled back down the hill, forcing him to repeat his effort—through all eternity.

This effectively happens to many, if not most, attempts to change an organization or introduce a new product. People work hard and are mystified when the results are unsatisfactory. The problem is almost always that they dealt with only one part of the system, which meant that the system (an organization, a market, a customer) was free to resist. Understanding systems and how to control them will make success far more likely. But absent system thinking and system strategy, you are doomed to live with the Sisyphus Syndrome.

Why do dynamic systems resist change? It is merely an attempt to maintain system equilibrium. For example, the earth is a self-regulating biochemical system that maintains equilibrium among an unlikely combination of chemical gases—nitrogen and oxygen, with traces of carbon dioxide, methane, and argon. The human body is also a self-regulating system, which tries to maintain a constant body temperature of 98.6 degrees Fahrenheit.

What about *your* organization? Because it is a system, it tries to maintain equilibrium. That is why the status quo rules and change is anathema. Whenever you try to introduce change in an organization, there is always system resistance. Indeed, the harder you push, the harder the system pushes back. Given that, it is not surprising that a number of organizational studies reveal a high failure rate for change initiatives—even though a majority of the individuals in the organization agree that new approaches are needed!

Systems have enormous resilience. Even when an organizational change strategy appears to succeed, the change is often temporary. The organization simply snaps back to the status quo when the external pressure stops. This is called the "Hysteresis Effect": Force applied against a material deforms it, but when you release the force, the material tends to return to its original position. The material "remembers" where it had been. To achieve permanent change you must exceed the system's "elastic limits."

Now apply this elastic-limits lesson to executing a strategy. Your strategy may call for you to make substantial changes in the products or services you produce, or to whom you sell them, or how you sell them—or all of the foregoing. These changes will certainly impact the equilibrium of the market in which you operate. They will also impact the equilibrium inside your own organization.

When you disrupt the system equilibrium, expect pushback. Most of your executives, employees, and department heads will resist any kind of change, regardless of how "good" it may be. And opposition won't stop at the walls of your organization. When you try to change the rules, your suppliers, competitors, and other components of the external system in which you operate will push back as well. Each system component will, consciously or unconsciously, place barriers in your path.

So the operative assumption is this: System resistance is like death and taxes. It *cannot* be avoided.

AFFECTING "CENTERS OF GRAVITY"

A winning strategy addresses the "enemy"—which is not a particular competitor in the market or some group advocating the status quo within your organization. The "enemy" is always the current system *as a whole*. To create the future, you must change the system.

Every system has leverage points—what we call "Centers of Gravity." By understanding what they are and how to affect them, you can rapidly and efficiently achieve seemingly impossible goals—system magic.

History is full of examples. Alexander the Great used the Center of Gravity approach to defeat a powerful opponent. When he embarked on his campaign against Persia, success depended on securing control of the Mediterranean Sea. However, there was a major problem: Alexander's fleet was too weak to overcome the Persian fleet and had no prospect of becoming significantly stronger. But Alexander understood that the Centers of Gravity of the Persian fleet were its shore bases. Before plunging into Persia, he used his land forces to seize Persian naval bases around the Mediterranean. Alexander destroyed Persian sea power without ever winning a single battle at sea.

The Prussian military theorist Carl von Clausewitz described a Center of Gravity as the "hub of all power and movement" in an opposing enemy line. This, he stated, is "the point against which all energies should be directed." He was right in his description but fatally wrong in thinking that a complex system (an army, a state) could be reduced to a single Center of Gravity. This error has led many of his adherents to make monumental errors in their military planning and operation.

Dynamic, complex systems, in fact, have *multiple* Centers of Gravity. In your organization, for example, you must deal with many every day—your competition, customers or clients, suppliers, key employees above and below you in the organization, systems like finance and marketing, and technology, to name a few. To get things done, you always need to move more than one of these Centers of Gravity in the desired direction—and the more you move in the least amount of time, the higher will be your probability of achieving lasting change.

Most game-changing business leaders intuitively grasp that there are multiple Centers of Gravity in their particular industries. Two decades ago, Bill Gates foresaw and attacked the multiple Centers of Gravity that would shape the emerging desktop computing market—personal computer users, corporate Information Technology personnel, third-party developers, distribution channels, and computer manufacturers. Gates built the biggest and most profitable software company in history, and in the process became, for a time at least, the richest man in America.

In 1997, Charles Schwab understood that the major Centers of Gravity in the emerging financial services market were the Internet, baby-boomers, and the financial press that large numbers of new investors read religiously. He executed a bold clicks-and-mortar plan to expand into a full-fledged Internet brokerage firm which, according to the *Los Angeles Times* in November 1999, had allowed it to bring in client assets "faster than any other brokerage firm in America." So much so that by 2000 Schwab, with one-fourth the workforce and one-tenth the revenue of full-service brokerage giant Merrill Lynch & Company, had generated a stock market capitalization almost as large as Merrill's. In our consulting work we have found that executives and managers who successfully lead change intuitively know what the Centers of Gravity are in their organizations. Their first order of business in a change effort is to "attack," these key Centers of Gravity personally and persistently: the board of directors, senior executives, key customers, and the informal rank-and-file leaders whom others tend to follow.

Many people will look at a Center of Gravity and immediately conclude that they are incapable of affecting it. They are wrong: Once you identify a Center of Gravity, there will be a way to affect it. Always.

Consider what the movie studio DreamWorks SKG did in its campaign to win the 2000 best-picture Oscar for its dark comedy *American Beauty.* In addition to the usual media "saturation bombing"—traditional broad-based advertising and publicity—DreamWorks SKG used a highly targeted approach aimed at the key Centers of Gravity of the Academy Awards: the 5,600 voters of the Academy of Motion Picture Arts and Sciences.

The strategy was a very precise attack on the Los Angeles–based Academy voters. Since direct-mail campaigning is specifically prohibited, the idea was to use a variety of locally aimed "smart bombs": a half-hour special on the making of *American Beauty* to be aired on Los Angeles cable channels; window displays in key bookstores around Los Angeles; "free" screenings for philanthropic organizations whose members also happened to be Academy voters.

There was also a bombardment of print advertisements, not just in big newspapers but also in the three trade papers—*Daily Variety, Weekly Variety,* and the *Hollywood Reporter.* Ads also appeared in small, free publications distributed in the areas where many academy members live, and there were targeted articles in small local magazines like *Back Stage West* (which is well-read by actors). Last but not least was a feature article in *Los Angeles* magazine's Hollywood issue, highlighted by a cover photo of the *American Beauty* actors wrapped in an American flag.

Since it is human nature to be influenced by personal contact, the campaign also included small group sessions and lots of personal appearances. According to the *Los Angeles Times,* a few weeks before the vote, a publicist took *American Beauty* screenwriter Alan Ball to Santa Barbara (where thirty to forty Academy voters reside) for a private dinner. "We figured five, ten, or twenty-five votes could make a difference," said the publicist.

In the final weeks before the vote, the *American Beauty* actors appeared on some key national television programs known to be favorites of Academy voters: Kevin Spacey on CBS's *60 Minutes* and on the Bravo cable channel's *Inside the Actors Studio;* Annette Bening on NBC's *The Tonight Show with Jay Leno,* and Sam Mendes, the director, on *CBS Sunday Morning.* Meanwhile MSNBC was running an hour-long special about the careers of Bening and Spacey.

All of this was designed to move the minds of the Academy voters in the desired direction. DreamWorks SKG played within the rules, but it left no Center of Gravity unturned in its precise, aggressive campaign.

The result was an Oscars sweep: The Academy of Motion Picture Arts and Sciences honored *American Beauty* not only with the best-picture award but four others: best director, best actor, best original screenplay, and best cinematography. Interestingly, a small eight-person PR team, one-third the size of the PR team of DreamWorks SKG's primary rival, Miramax, orchestrated this phenomenal effort.

THE PARALLEL APPROACH

There are two basic approaches to affecting Centers of Gravity: a) attack them serially, one step at a time; or b) attack them in parallel, taking many steps simultaneously.

There is a powerful argument against using the serial approach. Since it requires you to move in a step-by-step fashion, you must, by necessity, get each step right before you can move to the next one. In a ten-step process, if you optimistically project a 90 percent probability of success for each individual step, your overall probability of success is only about 35 percent. In short, you have a low probability of success when you move sequentially.

Anyone experiencing the frustration of Christmas lights on a series circuit understands the problem with a serial approach. In a series circuit, electricity must be able to pass through each bulb; if one is burned out, none light. You have to troubleshoot every bulb to find the problem. In business parlance, that's a lot of rework.

In a string of Christmas-tree lights wired in *parallel*, electricity flows separately to each bulb. Even if one or more has failed, you still have an overall positive result—the majority of the bulbs light up.

The same thing is true when a business campaign uses parallel operations. Single-point failures are not showstoppers. Because there are multiple Centers of Gravity, you have multiple opportunities to create the desired system impact. Perfect information and perfect execution are not nearly as important as they would be in a serial approach.

In short, when you take a parallel approach, you can afford to have some steps fail because a large percentage of other, simultaneous actions are succeeding. If the Desert Storm air campaign had succeeded in hitting only half the Center of Gravity targets designated for the first phase, the overall system impact would still have been sufficient.

What's more, the air campaign planners did not have to accurately predict the individual result of hitting each particular site. All they needed to predict was that the *overall* result of rapid, concerted hits on Saddam Hussein's palaces, command centers, and other key sites would sufficiently disrupt the Iraqi leadership structure.

That's exactly what happened. Saddam Hussein's top priority became not directing the war effort, but directing his personal safety effort! According to numerous postwar accounts, every night, just after the sun went down, Hussein would drive randomly around the Baghdad suburbs and then suddenly decide, "We will spend the night at this house." Fearing the Americans would intercept his communications and find him, he also instructed the people with him not to communicate his location or use their cell phones. The strategic result was that, for about half of each twenty-four-hour period, Iraq's "maximum leader" was incommunicado and unable to coordinate military operations.

The parallel approach has two essential elements: *multiplicity*—many Centers of Gravity are affected; and *simultaneity*—the effects occur at about the same time.

Consider this scenario. What would happen to the United States if, for a period of one year, one major city each week were struck by an earthquake? It would certainly create enormous problems, but the nation as a *whole system* has the resources to repair or work around major problems in one city per week. Now imagine what would happen if, simultaneously, 150 earthquakes hit 150 of the largest American cities—150 "Centers of Gravity," all of which are hubs of communications, transportation, and electricity. The whole system would go into shock. It is simply not capable of coping with that much concurrent damage.

Hard to imagine? Perhaps—but it's exactly what happened in the Persian Gulf War when those 150 Iraqi Centers of Gravity were assaulted during the first twenty-four hours. The effect of this high-speed, parallel approach was almost instantaneous and was rapidly catastrophic. There was simply no way the Iraqis could repair or even fully comprehend the damage. Parallel system impacts created chaos.

PARALLEL: ANTIDOTE TO RESOURCE LIMITATIONS

While people quickly see the enormous power of the parallel approach, they are often discouraged because they automatically assume that it will require substantially more resources—more people, more dollars, more time, more information—than they have available.

Actually, in the aggregate it will normally take less because of a phenomenon known as the "Time Value of Action" (Figure 4.1). The Time Value of Action tells us that our probability of success is increased significantly if we launch a concerted effort over a rela-

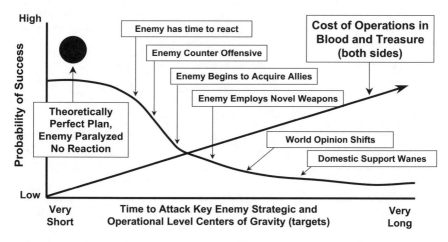

Figure 4.1 Time Value of Action—War

tively short period of time. As time goes by without success, our parallel efforts begin to fall apart, we revert to the serial world, and the probability of winning goes down rapidly.

Think of the very serial World War I with its increasingly bloody toll, compared to the Gulf War in which damage and death were very low—on both sides! In Figure 4.1, note that the highest probability of success occurs with the least expense, whereas the lowest probability is associated with very high costs.

In 1999 the world watched as NATO conducted a very serial war against Serbia for the first two months of the conflict. Serbia, although it suffered much damage to facilities, was unaffected as a system and was able to act on its own agenda. Only after NATO began to attack the whole Serbian system in a more parallel fashion did the Serbs collapse and agree to NATO terms. What was done in the third month of the war could have been done in the first week with a fraction of the resources and far less damage to Serbia.

The business case is identical. In Figure 4.2, we see that the likelihood of success for something like a new product introduction is far higher if all the key Centers of Gravity (from R&D to manufacturing to marketing) are affected in a very short period. Taking a

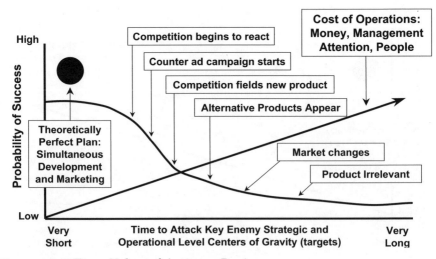

Figure 4.2 Time Value of Action—Business

long time to affect them—doing the job serially—can easily lead to complete failure, as depicted on the right side of the graph. In addition, as in the war example, the cost goes up over time while the probability of success falls significantly.

You've seen the "time is money" phenomenon again and again, especially in government. Whether it's mass transit or military aircraft, the programs stretch on and on while the expenses continue to rise. Invariably, there are costly reporting requirements and time-consuming administrative reviews. As the time frame stretches, individuals with critical project knowledge leave, which leads to even more delay and more cost. By the time the project is finished (if ever), it is hopelessly over budget and, worse, may no longer be relevant because so much has changed since its inception.

This "death by delay" phenomenon happens in the commercial sector as well as the government. The bankruptcy of Iridium, the satellite-based global phone service heavily backed by Motorola, is a vivid example of what can happen when you take too long and operate serially.

Iridium was a good idea, but it took nearly ten years from the concept to the completion of its sixty-six-satellite constellation. By then, as the *Los Angeles Times* described the event, "terrestrial wireless networks had evolved to the point that they could provide much of the service Iridium hoped to have to itself, and for far less than the $5 a minute Iridium charges. Even worse, Iridium's satellites, which were designed for the low-capacity demands of voice conversations but not for video and multimedia content, today look as obsolete as Edsels." Iridium marched smartly to the right side of Figure 4.2: The product became irrelevant.

There are other reasons why the parallel approach is cheaper and better. When you do things serially, you need very accurate information. Since the information you use to make decisions is rarely perfect, you end up making costly mistakes and doing many things more than once. In the parallel approach you don't have to do everything right. You just need to *make a critical mass of the right kinds of things happen quickly* so that the system moves in the direction you want.

The bottom line is this: A parallel approach, attacking multiple Centers of Gravity simultaneously, leverages your available resources to your best strategic advantage.

THE PARALLEL APPROACH IN BUSINESS

How does the principle of parallel attacks work in the marketplace? The global brand Pokémon targeted the youth market—specifically, young boys between the ages of six and twelve. Suddenly the brand was everywhere at once: a widely distributed movie; a cartoon show that aired eleven times each week on the Warner network; collectible trading cards; an ad blitz that included television, radio, and print ads; multiple Web sites that offered interactive components like "Pokedex," which helped kids track the toys they wanted to collect; promotional tie-ins with major organizations like Burger King; and, last but not least, a Nintendo video game.

The Gulf War had its Instant Thunder; we might call this "Instant Pokémon." If only half of these efforts worked, the result would still have been a huge success.

How does the parallel approach work *within* an organization? What's called concurrent engineering is in reality parallel design. Boeing Corporation used a parallel process to design and build from scratch an entirely new plane for the twenty-first century in record time. In 1991 Boeing made a board-level decision to place a huge bet on the company's ability to create and deliver one of the largest transport aircraft ever built, within four years—half the time that the process normally takes.

To accomplish this feat, the 777 became the first aircraft designed entirely on computer. Hundreds of engineers worked together in parallel, sharing designs in real time via sophisticated software called CATIA (computer-aided three-dimensional interactive application). In 1995 the very first 777 built flew on schedule, and the following year it went into commercial service. This breakthrough in design-cycle time would not have been possible without a parallel approach.

Almost by definition, you cannot make the right things happen quickly if you limit yourself to a serial approach. Because success in a warp-speed world depends on making the right things happen quickly, the parallel approach is a powerful approach that competitive companies must adopt; remaining in the serial world is a recipe for disaster.

No matter what the name—parallel processing, concurrency, parallel attack, market blitz, market saturation, simultaneous deployment—when you launch many precisely targeted actions, mostly against the right Centers of Gravity in a compressed time frame, the probability of success increases dramatically.

THE PROMETHIC LAWS

In this chapter we've explored the importance of Centers of Gravity and how to affect them. This is a systems approach to strategy built upon a solid foundation: a body of principles that we call the Promethic Laws. These laws describe a complete system-change cycle from beginning to end.

The Promethic Laws

- **Every action affects the future.** Every action has consequences that inexorably influence tomorrow. We cannot act and then think that nothing will happen because of our actions.
- **Specific actions create a specific future.** To define and create a desired future, you must take action. And the more specific the action, the more effective.
- **Everything and every action happens in a system.** Our bodies are systems as are our families, our companies, our markets, and our countries. Everything we do takes place in the context of one or more systems, and everything we do affects these systems in some way—and is affected by them.
- **All systems have inertia and resist change.** Newton long ago described the Law of Inertia: A body in motion tends to remain in motion; a body at rest tends to remain at rest. Systems follow a similar rule—they have inertia and resist change.

- **All systems have Centers of Gravity.** No matter how complex or how simple, every system has one or more components that exert a greater influence on the whole system than do other components. These "leverage points" are the system's Centers of Gravity. Change them, change the system.
- **Systems change when their Centers of Gravity change.** Systems may also change if enough elements that are not Centers of Gravity change, but the time and form of change become unpredictable. Important for our purposes, however, is to understand and accept the idea that system change is far more dependent on Center of Gravity change than on non–Center of Gravity change.
- **The extent and probability of system change is directly proportional to the number of Centers of Gravity affected and the speed at which they are affected.** If we affect a few Centers of Gravity and do so slowly, the system quickly learns how to repair itself. The key to overwhelming system opposition is the parallel approach: *multiplicity*—many Centers of Gravity are affected; and *simultaneity*—the effects occur at about the same time.
- **All known systems and things have a beginning and an end.** Everything around us functions in a cycle of some kind with a beginning and an end. Things will end. Period.
- **Specific actions produce specific ends.** If we know that everything will end, and we do, it would be irresponsible not to make the end as compatible with our desires as possible. This means that we must craft specific actions to create a specific end—just as we develop specific actions to create a specific future.

Chapter Debrief: Centers of Gravity

To create the future, you must transform the system. This means that every action, from new product to organization change, must address the entire system.

All dynamic systems vigorously resist change. You can overcome this resistance by focusing your resources in parallel against Centers of Gravity—the system's leverage points.

There are two basic approaches to affecting Centers of Gravity: serial and parallel.

Parallel is far better than serial because your chances of success are far higher: Fewer resources are required overall; you don't need perfect information; and you can afford to have some steps fail because a large percentage of other, simultaneous actions are succeeding.

Bottom line: The parallel approach accelerates results and increases the probability of success.

Prometheus Process

Now that you understand the theoretical underpinnings of Prometheus, we are ready to explore the process itself. It's built around four fundamental imperatives:

- The *Design the Future* imperative is about painting a clear and compelling picture of your destination, measuring strategic success, and defining the rules of conduct for the organization.
- The *Target for Success* imperative is about selecting the right targets for action using a powerful system model—what we will call, in Chapter 9, the "Five Rings"—and then defining the Desired Effects.
- The *Campaign to Win* imperative is about aggressively executing your system strategy. This is the phase of Prometheus in which you commission parallel campaigns and organize for success.
- The *Finish with Finesse* imperative is about an often-overlooked aspect of strategy—preparing for the inevitable ending of products, processes, and businesses. To remain a perennial winner, you must plan the endgame in advance.

The Four Imperatives

Design the Future	Target for Success	Campaign to Win	Finish with Finesse

Fig 4.3—The Four Imperatives

PROMETHEUS PROCESS

IMPERATIVE ONE

DESIGN THE FUTURE

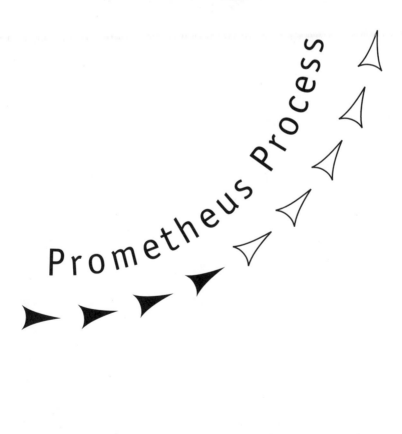

5

The Environment

"The future is not an optional event. Everyone will attend."

The first imperative of the Prometheus Process is to **Design the Future.** This begins with an understanding of the broad business, economic, and political context in which you will be operating. We refer to this as "scoping the environment."

What are the trends in your market space and in the wider world? How do these trends impact fundamental assumptions about who you are, what you do, and how you do it? What are the assumptions your associates are using as a basis of their proposals and decisions?

THE DIRECTION OF CHANGE

In today's hyper-speed environment, attempting to predict the specifics of the future is a fruitless, even counterproductive, exercise. One cartoon that sums up this problem shows a nervous businessman seated at a table with a fortune-teller, who is staring deeply into her crystal ball. He has an anxious look on his face as he awaits her prediction of the future. The caption reads, "I'm sorry, sir. The future is arriving faster than I can predict it!"

Although we can't predict specifics, we can certainly discern the *direction* of change—the macro-trends that affect virtually every aspect of our business and personal lives—and factor this knowledge into our planning.

Consider, for example, the trend in the processing power of computers. There is every reason to believe that Moore's Law (which says that storage capacity on microchips will double every eighteen months) will remain true. Indeed, it may actually understate future advances—even Mr. Moore himself thinks so. We are already seeing ever more powerful software and hardware that in turn spawn new tools that accelerate the process.

Accompanying the explosion in information technology are falling commodity prices; rapidly growing income and standard of living around the world; an ocean of venture capital money avail-

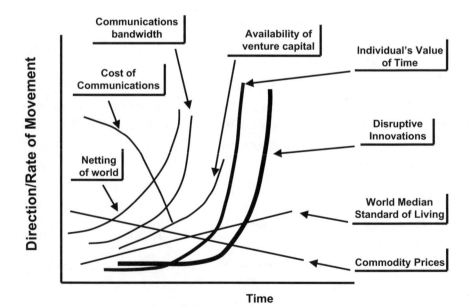

Figure 5.1—Hyper-Change

able to support almost any idea; and falling defense budgets that, one hopes, augur well for global peace and stability. There's been a rise in the value people place on their personal time, an increasingly scarce commodity that is shaping consumer choices in goods and services. And we're seeing what scholars call "disruptive" innovations and concepts—ideas and technologies that sharply change our expectations.

Taken together, these events create the complex new epoch suggested by Figure 5.1. How can we understand these developments? Three underlying historic seismic shifts simplify our understanding of what is happening: Time-Compression, Disruption, and Precision.

Each will have a dramatic impact on your future. Each will impact society in general as well as your market space. What opportunities or threats do they present for your business?

SEISMIC SHIFT: TIME-COMPRESSION

For most of human history, the tempo of life had a reassuring predictability. The expectation of what could be done in an hour or day or week was relatively constant. Time had a gold standard: the sun.

When the Industrial Age arrived in the nineteenth century, it brought with it a relentless drive to increase what could be done within a given time frame. It also introduced a new social malady: time pressure.

Today, the exponential increase in the number of significant events occurring within a given time frame is, in effect, compressing time; and with this time compression, the very nature of information itself is changing radically.

We've all seen countless examples of how operating by the timeframe assumptions of the past can be dangerous. For example, cycle time in manufacturing has been reduced dramatically. Michael Dell, CEO of Dell Computers, said in 1999 that his company kept a maximum of eight and a half days of inventory on hand for building computers. The reason: If the inventory time was any longer, his company would face technological obsolescence.

In earlier times, it must have been tough and frustrating to be an inventor, an innovator, or a discoverer. Many, many years usually had to drift by before a new product or service became widespread enough to have any kind of significant impact. Often the inventor failed to benefit from his invention—he was long dead and gone before the diffusion took place. Or else, by the time products using the new technology or idea were sufficiently developed to be practical, knowledge about the technology had spread so broadly that the originator's competitive advantage was lost. In yesterday's slow-moving environment, old and new technologies could exist side by side for long periods before the new finally supplanted the old. Examples include sailing ships and galleys; motorcars and horse transport; repeaters and muzzle loaders; electricity and gaslight.

Today, no one can any longer depend on the luxury of a long bell-shaped innovation curve that permits years of experimenting. The innovation curve must be compressed and squared if a new product or idea is to have real hope of success. What we always "knew" about product introduction and marketing may have already joined Aristotle's concept of an earthcentric universe.

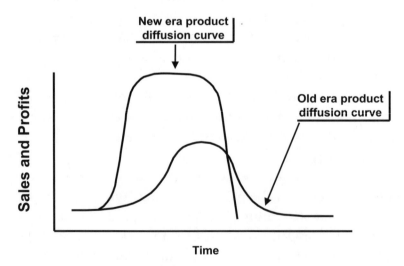

Figure 5.2 Product Diffusion

Is the familiar cycle of acceptance of new innovations still happening, but in compressed time? Or is there now a different model for introducing new products and services, a market driven by rapid and widespread availability of product information, user-friendly designs, and changing attitudes toward new ideas and new technology? If so, those operating under the old slow-time diffusion model will be falling behind the power curve, allowing more nimble competitors to capture the customers.

Many learned observers believe that all of this sends a message: We've seen the end of traditional business cycles. Others believe we're witnessing the same business cycles, but with their time frames compressed from years and months to weeks and days. In other words, the same dynamics are there, but occurring at a far faster rate.

Regardless of who is right, the time frames of business and economic measures need to be reexamined. In today's environment, are months and quarters the right time frames for corporate financial reports? In some instances, would weeks or days (or even hours!) be more appropriate?

To be a long-term winner, an organization must come to grips with the reality of time compression. It's not only the cycle times of your business processes that need a reality check, but also the mind-set of your people. The Time Value of Action—the faster you move, the higher your probability of success—should be ingrained in the organization's genetic code.

SEISMIC SHIFT: DISRUPTIVE INNOVATIONS

With time frames growing ever shorter, the incumbents in mature markets no longer enjoy a huge advantage simply because they have been around for a while and are familiar to customers. It's hard to imagine a mature market that is not going to come under furious attack by someone with a radically new idea or process.

For cutting-edge companies that have driven new markets from infancy to maturity, the risks are also significant. The rules in new markets are still being written, and they can change quickly and significantly. Whether an organization is in a mature or a new market, its competitive edge can disappear in a flash when a new competitor arrives on the scene. So the message is that you cannot rest on your laurels. As Intel Chairman Andy Grove points out, "Only the paranoid survive." Bill Gates has another way of describing this phenomenon: "In three years, every product my company makes will be obsolete. The only question is whether we'll make them obsolete or somebody else will."

The near-universal availability of information drives a tidal wave of new innovations, and many of these will be *disruptive* innovations—new technologies, products, and business models that change the competitive rules overnight.

In his book *The Innovator's Dilemma,* Clayton Christensen debunks a popular myth: Well-established firms fail because they are too stupid to grasp the import of new technologies. How often have we heard about the buggy-whip makers who refused to see that the automobile would destroy their businesses? Christensen showed that, in instance after instance, leading companies were well aware of the new technologies arising around them. But they had an almost impossible problem: They were captives of their customers, who insisted on marginal changes to existing products and typically rejected radical new products.

Christensen also makes clear that survival in a disrupted industry is statistically rare. For example, virtually all the companies that made the great commercial sailing ships of the nineteenth century failed to make a transition to power propulsion. In other words, incumbents actually listen closely to their customers—too closely.

The lesson here is, "When it comes to planning your future, don't listen too closely to your mainstream customers."

Because they don't want radical change, they will rarely embrace a disruptive innovation. What mainstream customers want initially is incremental innovation within the current technology paradigm. While they understand the need to migrate toward ever-better products and services, there is a natural resistance to anything that requires new strategies or new business models. In short, a product or service that disturbs the market system is often difficult to commercialize with mainstream customers.

In a hyper-change climate, what are the chances of your organization being affected by a disruptive innovation? The chances are very high, and getting higher because of the accelerating pace of innovation.

How can you tell which new products and services might pose a legitimate threat in your market space? Taking a snapshot of an innovation's current capabilities won't tell you that. You have to look forward to the future and ask, "What are my customers *really* looking for? Why do they buy what I sell? Could an alternative fill that space?" If the answer is yes—no matter how far-fetched the possibility, no matter how loyal your customers—a potential disruption is in the making.

SEISMIC SHIFT: REVOLUTIONARY PRECISION

The third seismic shift, revolutionary precision, showed its potential for extraordinary impact during the Desert Storm campaign—perhaps one of the most vivid examples of this seismic shift at work.

In World War II, to have a 90 percent probability of dropping one bomb from the workhorse B-17 on a target about a third the size of a football field required dropping 9,000 bombs. This meant putting a thousand aircraft and 10,000 men at risk in order to have 90 percent probability that one bomb would fall into that size target.

In every war up to that time, most weapons and projectiles missed their targets, so the job of the commander was essentially managing misses and trying to succeed in a statistically impossible environment.

In the Gulf War, everything changed. One bomb, one airplane, one pilot had the same probability of success that 9,000 bombs and 10,000 men had in World War II. That is a four order-of-magnitude change in precision. Overnight, the problem for commanders shifted from managing misses to managing hits—a shockingly different task.

The same kind of precision revolution is now occurring in the world of e-commerce. For example, the strategy of the major booksellers in the past was to build large bookstores in many different locations and stock them with many different kinds of books, in the hope that when you walked into one of the stores, you would find what you were looking for. Just like World War II bombing, it seemed perfectly reasonable at the time; but today, the large corner bookstore is looking more and more like a very imprecise and costly way to do business.

Today, Amazon.com operates a virtual facility employing precision search engines, allowing customers to find the exact book they want, instantly. Moreover, the automated software can give some tightly targeted information associated with the book they're considering, such as reader reviews and which related books have been bought by customers who bought this book.

The Web-based auctions offer another e-commerce example of the precision revolution. eBay and its imitators allow a multitude of buyers to rapidly decide what something is really worth. What we're witnessing is a revolution in which buyers and sellers separated by hundreds or thousands of miles, or on opposite sides of the globe, can conduct precise business transactions in nanoseconds.

The seismic shift toward revolutionary precision is not limited to the technology-driven Internet world. It's also occurring in the realm of business processes, perhaps best exemplified by the familiar "Six Sigma" program. Based on the concept of sigma, a measure statisticians use to refer to the variability of a process, the Six Sigma program aims to achieve a quality level in which failures occur at the rate of only 3.4 times per million opportunities.

Typical companies in the manufacturing-and-services industry accept 3.5 to 4.0 sigma performance levels as the acceptable norm, despite the fact that this means between 6,000 and 23,000 defects per million opportunities. These were the quality standards established in the second decade of the twentieth century—an era when it was assumed that only a certain level of process precision was possible or even economically feasible.

Six Sigma is not twice better than three sigma; it's ten thousand times better! The drive for such order-of-magnitude improvements in processes was pioneered by Motorola in the 1980s, when it began to explore the real cost of poor quality. It found, through extensive global benchmarking, that when a company operates at a

3.5 to 4.0 sigma level of precision, it spends on average about 10 percent of its gross revenue fixing mistakes. More recent estimates say the cost for this level of imprecision ranges from 20 to 30 percent of gross sales. Contrast that with the cost of fixing mistakes when operating at Six Sigma: close to 1 percent. The dollar savings are clearly huge.

Today, this precision revolution is building momentum. The man who led General Electric for twenty years, CEO Jack Welch, became a standard-bearer for Six Sigma. His motivation: General Electric estimated that the gap between three or four sigma and Six Sigma was costing it between seven billion and ten billion dollars per year. Other highly respected and successful companies have also applied Six Sigma principles with extraordinary success; five years into its Six Sigma effort, AlliedSignal reported savings of over two billion dollars.

When Motorola moved toward Six Sigma, it not only reduced costs attributable to quality problems, but it also raised employee productivity and morale (who wants to spend his life on reworks?) and reduced cycle times for product development dramatically.

Six Sigma applies in manufacturing, customer service, and every other aspect of all businesses. The real lesson is this: You can no longer afford to "miss," and the tools and concepts to "hit" with precision are now available. The real challenge, however, is the shift in mind-set to managing hits, understanding that misses are no longer a necessity.

ADDRESSING ASSUMPTIONS

As we get ready to begin the Prometheus Process of strategic thinking, planning, and execution, we need to ensure that everyone in our organization knows about the seismic shifts. Some people will be less convinced than others, but that is acceptable up to a point as long as we are aware of their thinking.

Among the many errors people and organizations make as they try to plan for the future is a failure to understand the operative assumptions of everyone who will have an impact on the success or failure of the plan. In laying the groundwork for the Prometheus Process, it's essential to find out what people are thinking about the future. We are not so much interested in having a party-line view as in knowing that everyone knows everyone else's assumptions and perspectives.

An example of the insight this effort can bring: The "financial people" are loath to borrow money to support what everyone knows is a great project, and everyone associated with the project agrees the financial people are shortsighted and don't understand the opportunities. It may turn out, however, that they do understand the opportunities but are concerned that interest rates are going to collapse in a matter of weeks, after which the company can borrow at a much lower cost. Meanwhile they assume everyone else shares their assumption about the future.

Again, it doesn't matter whether everyone agrees on the assumptions. Merely knowing *why* people are making their decisions goes a long way toward promoting the kind of trust and harmony important for business success.

We have found it useful to capture people's macro-assumptions in the following areas. You won't have all the answers, but thinking through the questions will help you design your organization's future:

Economic Environment: Will interest rates rise or fall substantially? Will there be a significant recession or depression? Will the stock market rise or fall substantially or will it remain flat?

Marketplace Dynamics: Will the markets in which you have an interest see major structural changes? Is consolidation likely? Are there new products or services on the horizon that would radically change your market? Will distribution patterns change significantly?

Political Environment: Will there be a change in control of the White House or in federal and state legislatures? Are new regulations likely that would change your business? Is there likely to be a major change in tax policy that would affect your markets? If you are operating overseas or intend to do so, what political changes do you assume there?

Sea Changes: Are any sea changes on the horizon? (Sea changes are those dramatic moments at sea when wind and wave patterns alter radically, either ending a terrible storm, plunging you into one, or changing one kind of storm into another.) In this case, we want to know if anyone thinks anything is going to happen that might carry you into a radically different world.

Technological Environment: Are there technological changes under way or likely to be that will allow you to do business in a different way or that will materially threaten the way you are currently doing business?

Other Assumptions: Does anybody have any other assumptions that they believe might affect the enterprise?

Again, the purpose of this exercise is not to predict the future or to correct "erroneous" assumptions on anyone's part; rather, it is simply for everyone to hear the macro-assumptions that other people are using to make general and specific business decisions. Knowing how people are thinking, and having a feel for how many of them share particular assumptions, is a powerful first step in planning.

THE MEANING OF "SCOPING THE ENVIRONMENT"

As we've seen, before launching into the Prometheus Process, it is essential to define expectations about the world in which you will be operating. To reiterate: Succeeding in a revolutionary time requires that you think like a revolutionary.

In this exciting, challenging business environment, everything except ethical values must be on the table, ready for discard or major modification. The opportunities are here, but those who ignore the changes sweeping every corner of the globe will not realize them.

No one can escape the realities of revolutionary change, and indeed no one should wish to, as it brings the opportunity for unprecedented wealth even to places where people have never known a life that goes beyond basic subsistence.

Chapter Debrief: The Environment

Although we can't predict specifics of the future, we can certainly discern the direction of change—the macro-trends that affect virtually every aspect of our business and personal lives—and factor this knowledge into our planning.

There are three seismic shifts under way that will affect virtually every business:

- An exponential increase in the number of significant events occurring within a given time frame.
- A tidal wave of disruptive innovations—new technologies, products, and business models that change the competitive rules overnight and put market incumbents out of business.
- The pursuit of revolutionary precision in technology-driven transactions and in the realm of business processes.

6

The Future Picture

"Work back from the future—not forward from the present."

If anyone suggested that we set sail with no idea where we were going and no beacon to guide us, few would sign aboard. To be truly enthusiastic about a journey, we must believe that the ship upon which we sail has a desirable destination.

In the Prometheus Process, that desirable destination is called the "Future Picture"—a clear and compelling description of what you want reality to be at some point in the future.

Once you have "scoped the environment" and come to an understanding of the overall context in which you'll be operating, it's time to put flesh on that skeleton by defining the specific elements that will compose your Future Picture.

This future should be as far ahead as possible, but not so far that it seems irrelevant for the stakeholders. For a project team, three to five months may be about right; for most businesses, three to five years is often appropriate. For nations, it could be decades or more. In any event, it should be sufficient to give the organization a beacon for the duration of at least the current business and technology cycles, and should prepare it to deal with the next ones.

You might be thinking, "It's hard to know what to expect that far ahead in today's turbulent environment."

The speed and complexity of change is precisely why you need an overarching Future Picture. When it has luminance and resolution, the Future Picture can be a valuable navigational aid, a constant beacon toward which everyone in the organization can steer. They may encounter fair winds or foul, but as they deal with the weather of the moment, everyone can still see the destination.

Since the Future Picture defines only where you are headed, and not the how-to-get-there details, it allows you to be "unyieldingly flexible"—constant in your ultimate destination, yet adaptable in terms of the exact course you will follow. In short, you have the creative space to define new ways of doing business, to build new competencies, and to set new standards within the framework of the Future Picture.

A winning Future Picture tends to push the envelope. Boldness has a very practical benefit, stretching people's thinking and causing everyone to be extraordinarily resourceful. At the dawn of the E-Commerce Age, for example, Jeff Bezos pictured his company as "the Earth's biggest seller of everything." Aiming high, he intended to put Amazon.com at the center of the on-line retailing universe. Bezos's Future Picture did more than launch a successful company: It revolutionized the retailing industry.

It's important to recognize that even the best Future Pictures have a finite life span. The great railroads that flourished in the nineteenth century because of their exorbitantly spectacular Future Picture—ribbons of iron across a continent, carrying the people and products of a booming industrial revolution—mostly perished in the next century. They failed to create a *new* Future Picture to deal with a new strategic cycle in technology and commerce.

Painting the Future Picture is the most critical step in planning your Grand Strategy. It is the genesis. All subsequent decisions and actions will be based upon it. If you get your Future Picture wrong, you can be making a costly mistake. You'll end up going down dead-end paths and missing big opportunities.

That's what happened to Wang Laboratories. During the 1970s and 1980s, Wang was a winner, successfully introducing several disruptive innovations: word processing, document imaging, and DP/telephony integration, among others. Yet Wang went into a steep decline in the late 1980s and filed for bankruptcy in 1992. What went wrong? Wang's original Future Picture—to be the leading R&D center in proprietary office systems—was too limiting. The company became obsolete overnight when the open-architecture PC emerged.

A winning Future Picture for Wang would have been "to remain the leading R&D center in office technology." Given that kind of context, the company's research on market trends would have been broader, and the leadership would probably have recognized and included personal computers in its R&D program.

ARCHITECTURAL THINKING

By far the best way to create a Future Picture—and every other element of your strategy—is to use a back-from-the-future approach we call "Architectural Thinking."

Let's assume you're building a house. Your architect won't overload you in the beginning with a lot of details about what materials are available, but rather he will begin "at the top" with some high-level questions: "What kind of house are you thinking about? What style appeals to you?" Once he has a sense of your overall aesthetic preferences, the architect will go into a bit more detail. "How many children do you have? What are their ages? How many drivers are in the family?" The questions will then move to your lifestyle: "Do you work at home? What kinds of hobbies do you have? How often do you entertain?" He will ask about taste and personal choices: "Do you prefer a formal or informal setting? Would you like a conservatory? An exercise room?"

Soon the architect will return with one or several suggestions for the layout of the house. Once you come to an agreement on the layout, he will create a detailed set of plans that can be sent out to contractors for bidding and for actual construction.

Think of your Future Picture as an architectural view of the new organization you are going to build. A Future Picture is a high-resolution view of what your organization will look like at some point in the future. It is measurable, and it can be acted upon. It is not a typical vision with flowery statements about being the best in this or that. It is real. It is compelling. It is what will happen if many people participate in its development and accept it as their future as well as that of their organization. It covers all facets of the organization.

KEY DESCRIPTORS—THE COMPONENTS OF A FUTURE PICTURE

When architects design homes, they recognize that the size and layout of the different rooms will vary immensely from one client to the next depending upon needs and personal preferences, but the categories of rooms will be very much the same.

Likewise for designing the future of any kind of organization. Specifics will vary, but the categories of the "rooms" are similar.

We have identified twelve categories for a Future Picture, which we call "Key Descriptors," that fit businesses large and small, start-up or mature, high tech or low tech. These descriptors are:

Financial Position: Where do you want the organization to be financially at a specified point in the future? Your answer should focus on the *value* you want the organization to have. The value might be a market capitalization for a publicly traded company, or it might be what someone would pay to buy the company if it is privately held.

Market Position: Do you want to operate as a commodity business? Or should you be highly differentiated? Do you intend to create, drive, or trail the market? (Trailing can, of course, be a perfectly valid strategy).

Business Areas: What business areas do you want to be in? What areas would make long-term strategic sense? This may include all or only some of the business areas you are currently involved in. It may even mean moving into a *new* business area.

Innovation: Do you intend to be first to market with new, commercially viable products? Or do you want your innovation efforts to be primarily for continuous improvement of current products? Does innovation even make sense for your business?

Stakeholder Perception: How do you want to be seen by your stakeholders—your officers and employees, your board, your customers, and your suppliers?

Outsider Perception: How do you want to be seen by people outside your company? You should consider the view that you want investment analysts, media, the community, and other companies in the industry to have of your organization.

Workforce Characteristics: What do you want your employees and associates to be like? Entrepreneurial? Innovative? Consistent? Cautious?

Brand: Do you want to have a brand? If so, for what do you want it to stand, and how widely do you want it to be known?

Corporate Culture: Are you satisfied with the current working environment? If not, what do you want to change? What kind of environment do you intend to have?

Corporate Citizenship: Do you want to take an active role in community or charitable affairs? As a company? As individuals?

Incentive Philosophy: What kind of an incentive program do you want—one in which profit-sharing or equity play major roles, or one in which salary or wages are dominant?

Ownership: Do you want to be a privately or publicly held corporation? If you want to be privately held, would you consider forming or acquiring publicly held companies in which you have an appropriate share?

People often ask, "Which of the Key Descriptors are most important?" These are not stand-alone characteristics. The various descriptors in your Future Picture are like the different colors of paint, different shapes, and different brushstroke patterns an artist uses in creating a portrait, still life, or landscape.

Which colors or shapes in the painting are most important? The answer is that you really cannot differentiate among them. If you take some of them away, you substantially change the look and feel of the overall painting.

THE FUTURE PICTURE STATEMENT

Once the responses to the Key Descriptor questions have been carefully thought out, the answers are synthesized in a Future Picture statement. As an example, here is a Future Picture statement for the hypothetical FastWin Corporation, a $600 million manufacturer and distributor of medical devices.

THREE-YEAR FUTURE PICTURE FOR FASTWIN CORPORATION

Key Descriptors Statements

Key Descriptor CATEGORY	Key Descriptor STATEMENT
FINANCIAL POSITION	FastWin will have a market capitalization twice its current size, and remuneration of employees will have increased in direct proportion to its success in making this financial position a reality.
MARKET POSITION	FastWin will be a market driver and leader.
BUSINESS AREAS	FastWin will continue to manufacture and market high-margin medical devices for professional caregivers. It also will explore opportunities in the self-care medical market.
INNOVATION	FastWin will continue to innovate in technology and business processes, products, and services that will have

	quantum effects on business results at every level.
STAKEHOLDER PERCEPTION	FastWin's stakeholders will see the organization as a smart place to invest their time, energy, and money.
OUTSIDER PERCEPTION	FastWin will have a reputation as a solid financial performer that offers high-quality, leading-edge products.
WORKFORCE CHARACTERISTICS	FastWin will have a highly productive, entrepreneurial workforce.
BRAND	The FastWin brand will be the gold standard in the medical device industry.
CORPORATE CULTURE	FastWin will have an open culture that encourages smart risk-taking.
CORPORATE CITIZENSHIP	FastWin will help select communities to acquire the latest medical technology.
OWNERSHIP	FastWin will remain a public company with substantial stock ownership by its employees.
INCENTIVE PHILOSOPHY	FastWin will reward results, recognize activity, and make many of its employees rich.

"Painting" each of these Key Descriptors is a creative process that is enhanced by the right perspective. It helps to keep these pointers in mind:

- **Think about the possibilities of tomorrow.** From the freedom of that vantage point, define your desired outcome—an ideal end result—for each Key Descriptor.
- **Define high-level outcomes.** Be very clear that the picture you are painting is your true end result and not simply a tactic.

- **Unleash your creativity.** Temporarily suspend your assumptions about what you think is feasible, and push the envelope. Make a relatively unconstrained choice about what you want to happen, rather than projecting what you currently assume to be possible.
- **Be optimistic.** People who are in a positive frame of mind are more cognitively flexible—capable of thinking in new ways—than people in a neutral or negative frame of mind.
- **Be specific.** Clarity is power, so don't accept fuzziness. The more specifically the Key Descriptors are stated, the clearer and more achievable the Future Picture will be.

It's very important that a critical mass of your key stakeholders—even investors, if you can find a way to do this—participate in this process. The benefit is not only a better Future Picture, but also a much higher probability that it will be achieved.

There are several reasons why this is true. You are able to construct a much more complete and "buyable" Future Picture when you consider the aspirations of all your stakeholders. Because there is an open sharing of ideas and information among the participants, everyone's perspective expands. During the implementation phase, there will be a much higher level of cross-functional collaboration because of the insights participants gain during the planning process about parts of the organization other than their own. And people will make faster and better decisions during execution because they understand the nuances of where the organization is going, and why.

THE IDEAL FINAL RESULT

Project teams can also create a Future Picture for a specific product or service using an approach called the "Ideal Final Result." First conceived in 1946 by Genrich Altshuller, a brilliant young thinker in the former Soviet Union, the Ideal Final Result concept has spread around the world.

Picture the most perfect product imaginable—and then work back as necessary to something that can be done. Like the larger concept of the Future Picture, this approach allows you to escape biases of the present.

One of our colleagues, Dr. Andrei Aleinikov, who teaches organizations to use the Ideal Final Result approach, explains it this way:

> You can imagine an Ideal Final Result in any situation. For example, the Ideal Final Result in transportation is no physical vehicle. The *Star Trek* transporter is close to that ideal—"Beam me up, Scotty!"
>
> A food service company thinking about the perfect product for its consumer customers might see the Ideal Final Result as one where whatever tasty meal the customer envisaged appears in front of him—and payment flowed instantly into the providing company's coffers.
>
> Of course, this ideal may be unrealizable in practice. Nevertheless, by considering the ideal first you greatly expand the scope of your thinking—and begin to think the unthinkable!

So, when you start a new product development project, use the Ideal Final Result as a model for conceptualizing. Assume you can make something that will not break, that needs no maintenance, and that will make the customer smile with every use. The results are often amazing.

And, of course, you will use the same kind of thinking for every other type of project and effort as well.

OPEN PLANNING: THE POWER OF NUMBERS

A vital tool for creating your Future Picture is one we've mentioned earlier: Open Planning. The origin of Open Planning was serendipitous, growing out of urgent need. When John Warden was called on to develop an air plan for General Schwarzkopf in two days, he knew he faced a nearly impossible challenge. John later recalled his thinking:

> I briefly considered gathering a very small group of peo-
> ple around me, closing the doors, and doing it all in great
> secrecy. Quickly, however, I realized that this didn't make
> much sense—I was certainly no expert on Iraq, I needed a
> lot of help, but I didn't even have a way of knowing who or
> what I needed.
>
> I decided to open the doors of a big briefing room we
> had in the basement of the Pentagon and gather as many
> people as possible.
>
> Right from the start, everyone in the group was
> involved in almost everything that took place. This way,
> everybody understood not only the decisions but also the
> thinking and discussions associated with them. So they
> were able to do most of their work without reference to any
> higher authority, secure in the knowledge they were doing
> the right thing.

Most of us have grown up in organizational environments where only certain selected people take part in important discussions. The results of these meetings rarely get translated in enough detail and with enough nuance to allow those who didn't participate to understand the thinking well enough. So they lack the understanding needed to make smart decisions on their own—which they must do if movement is not to be glacial.

GUIDELINES FOR OPEN PLANNING

How do you go about applying the Open Planning approach in creating your Future Picture?

The ideal planning group would be everyone—hardly practical in any sizable organization. We've found that a group size of fifty to seventy works well. It's desirable, though of course not always possible, to have all key members of management attend. And invite a handful of very junior people, as well. At the very start, impress on everyone that they are not attending to protect existing structures and practices. Also, they're not attending to represent any other group or person but are participating in their own right.

It may sound impossible to get anything done with more than a few people; on the contrary, the participation of many people makes the chore move faster and makes successful execution more likely. Large groups become impossible only when they are allowed to discuss *tactics,* because there are usually hundreds if not thousands of tactics with equal validity.

Instead, require everyone to work at a *strategic* level. If you're using the Prometheus Process, the methodology provides a template for discussion and forces strategic-level thinking.

The leader of the group should be someone comfortable with the Prometheus Process and committed to using it. If the subject is the Grand Strategy for the organization, the leader should be the business owner or CEO. It's imperative that the senior people in the organization be present and that they participate.

CLOSED-DOOR VS. OPEN-DOOR PLANNING

When doors are open, there is a greater likelihood that the plan will be successfully executed. It's only common sense: A larger number of people understand the nuances of the plan and have a sense of ownership.

Think about the "closed-door" planning approach used by most organizations. A few people—usually some senior executives working in a small team—develop a strategic plan. With fewer participants, there is a higher risk that something important will be ignored. Nonetheless, once its work is complete, the team explains it to the rest of the organization and tries to convince people to buy in. More often than not, there is system resistance—the vast majority of people remain skeptical and unwilling to support something they don't fully understand or own. This lack of understanding and buy-in is one of the major reasons why strategies fail during the execution phase.

There are, of course, some leaders who are uncomfortable with the "messiness" of Open Planning, regardless of the advantages. They object to moving fast because it means not having perfect information; or they're afraid that if they open the planning process to a large number of people, "things will get out of control."

Certainly, Open Planning is not a button-down affair and it requires a bit more time on the front end. But overall, Open Planning is a time-*saver*. Because a critical mass of people understands and support the plan, they tend to move faster, and make better decisions when it comes time to implement. In short, "If *we* build it, *we* will come."

Openness does not end with the Future Picture phase. To ensure fast, aligned execution of the plan, it should be clearly communicated and vetted with everyone in the organization. Some leaders respond to this idea with moral indignation. "How dare you suggest something like that in such a competitive environment!"

One of our colleagues tells a story that makes this point. A senior vice president of a major telecommunications firm had just come up with a new strategic plan. As soon as it was finished, he printed up copies of the plan to circulate to everybody in the business unit. The night before it was to be distributed, his boss, one of the top officers of the organization, called him and asked in an outraged tone of voice, "What the devil are you doing? I heard you're going to publish your strategic plan. If you give the plan to everybody in your business unit, it will be a catastrophe! Do you realize the security implications? One of our competitors could get a copy and know what we're doing!"

The executive who had led the development process was astounded. "Let me make sure I understand the logic here. You are saying we shouldn't communicate the plan to everyone in the organization because some competitor might learn about it. So the smart thing to do is not to tell the people on our team what the plan is. Is that it?" His boss responded, "That's exactly what I'm saying!"

This Open Planner left his organization shortly thereafter to head up a new company—one that in just four years saw its market capitalization multiply by a factor of five while his previous company became worth substantially less over the same period

FUTURE PICTURE: STAYING THE COURSE

Once you have agreed on a Future Picture, you should be very careful about changing it. To return to the sailing metaphor, what would happen if you changed your destination every time the winds changed? When the winds start to blow southwest, you suddenly decide that Cape Town, South Africa, is really a better destination because you can get there faster. However, after a few days, the winds begin to blow due north. So you now decide that Reykjavík, Iceland, looks good.

Consider the impact this kind of free-floating Future Picture has on an organization. As a description of the ultimate destination, the Future Picture is supposed to be the beacon that enables synchronized planning and execution. When that beacon doesn't exist or its location changes with the prevailing winds, people with the best of intentions go off in different directions, trying to maximize their own tactical efforts. Alignment is absent and people work at cross-purposes—not because they mean to be counterproductive, but because they have no way to know how they can work together. The result: The whole is less than the sum of its parts.

A clear, consistent Future Picture has enormous power. Ronald Reagan vividly demonstrated this during his presidency. Whether they voted for him or not, most people would agree that Reagan had a clear and consistent vision for America. Understanding Reagan's vision, the thousand or so people who worked in the White House stayed on the same page.

Once you've decided on your destination, the next step is to *engrave the Guiding Precepts*—the rules and behavior that will guide you on the road to the future.

Chapter Debrief: Future Picture

Painting the Future Picture means creating a clear and compelling description of where you want to be at some point in the future.

The Future Picture is the most critical element in your strategy. It is the genesis. All subsequent decisions and actions will be based upon it.

By far the best way to create a Future Picture is to use Open Planning and a back-from-the-future approach called "Architectural Thinking."

The Future Picture should be as far ahead as possible, and should stretch people's thinking and cause them to be extraordinarily resourceful.

The various Key Descriptors in your Future Picture are like the different colors, different shapes, and different brushstroke patterns in a painting. All of them are important.

Since the Future Picture defines only where you are headed, and not the how-to-get-there details, it allows you to be "unyieldingly flexible"—constant in your ultimate destination, yet adaptable in the exact course line you will follow

A Future Picture, once determined, should be changed only under compelling circumstances.

Every Future Picture has a finite life span.

7

Guiding Precepts

"Know what you're willing to do."

There is an unspoken expectation that good people will do the "right thing" for the organization in their day-to-day work. But what exactly does it mean to do the "right thing"?

One way to do the "right thing" is to make every decision with the Future Picture in mind. "Will this action, this decision, move us closer or further away from our Future Picture?" Thinking long-term and keeping your eyes on the prize is critically important.

But people need to consider more than just the end result. Decisions should also reflect the core beliefs of an organization—its philosophy and character. The more clearly these beliefs are spelled out, the better.

Whether or not core beliefs are formally articulated, they are often visible in the collective behavior of the organization. Throughout history, organizations have exhibited the full range of behaviors, from nearly pure good to nearly pure evil. Mother Teresa's missionaries in Calcutta demonstrate a commitment to compassionate behavior of the highest level. But there have also been organizations that were totally amoral, like the Communists during the Russian revolution in 1917 who subscribed to the maxim "The end justifies the means."

What kind of behavior do you expect in your organization? What ideals and style are important to you? These questions need to be answered early on in your planning process—right at the same time you are painting your Future Picture. Clearly articulating behavioral expectations is a key aspect of designing the future.

Some leaders don't understand the importance of this. While working on the issue with one of our client companies, a top-ranking executive impatiently challenged, "Why are we wasting time on this stuff? We believe in empowerment. Just let the people do what they want. All I care about is results!"

What happens when a leader makes such a pronouncement? Do people think, "Great! Let's get going!" On the contrary, we've found that when the ground rules are fuzzy or nonexistent, people rarely think and act in *FastTime;* rather than taking immediate action, they tend to remain hesitant, worried that they will make the wrong decisions. The truth is that they really don't believe the pronouncement that they can "do what they want."

People know there are boundaries and behavioral expectations, even if their leaders haven't taken the time to define them. They assume that, if they unwittingly violate these mysterious rules, there will be consequences ranging from mild disapproval to job loss. The assumption is correct. There are always rules, whether spoken or unspoken.

Even though it takes some time to spell out the ground rules, it is time well spent. Without clearly defined standards of behavior, some negative things are likely to happen. Well-meaning individuals will take actions, make decisions, and treat each other and customers as they see fit, based on their own notions about what is important. Decisions and actions will be more heavily affected by short-term thinking and the emotions of the moment, and the potential for conflict among employees, managers, and executives will be higher, when there are no clearly agreed-upon ground rules.

The truth is that people *want* the ground rules to be clarified—

not to the point of dictating their every move, but with enough specificity about the boundaries and expectations to enable their creativity and enthusiasm to flourish. Microsoft COO Bob Herbold has described the attitude at that company as "a very unusual mix of knowing when it is that we have to be disciplined and march to one drummer, and when it is that we need to turn on the creative juices and be innovative. There is a lot of pride in this company," he has said, "in the efficiency of our decision-making."

ENGRAVING A GUIDING PRECEPT

Intel is a good example of the power of spelling out the ground rules. It encapsulated one of its key behavioral expectations in just two words: *Deliver innovation.*

In its early days, Intel was just one of a crowd of start-ups in the new world of transistors. How did it come to dominate the industry? Intel not only had a compelling Future Picture that defined its role in creating the technologies of tomorrow, it also had an intense core belief about what would differentiate it in the marketplace: the consistent ability to transform innovative ideas into practical products that met the needs of its customers.

Unlike most of its competitors that focused exclusively on product innovation, Intel based its differentiation on delivering market-driving new products. Its emphasis on delivering innovation led to balancing product innovations with the exigencies of putting its products into customers' hands: meeting schedules, lowering costs, improving distribution, expanding the range of products, and providing customer support, documentation, and technical development tools.

The way Intel embedded an intense commitment to "deliver innovation" into its organizational mind-set is an excellent example of *engraving Guiding Precepts.*

What is a Guiding Precept? It is a behavioral touchstone, a short statement about what is or what is not permissible behavior as people go about the work of achieving the Future Picture.

An effective Guiding Precept meets two conditions. First, it states in the clearest possible terms something that is considered to be of the highest philosophical or operational importance. Second, to the greatest extent possible, it is differentiating. The Guiding Precept that Intel engraved into the mind-set of its employees—"deliver innovation"—not only communicated the overriding importance of this behavior to the people inside the organization, but clearly differentiated Intel from its competitors in the marketplace.

When eloquently stated, Guiding Precepts can have a measurable impact on the behavior of large numbers of people over an extended period of time. Consider the long-term impact of the Declaration of Independence made by the thirteen American colonies. This remarkable document is inspiring even today with such powerful statements as, "We hold these truths to be self-evident, that all men are created equal, that they are endowed by their Creator with certain unalienable Rights, that among these are Life, Liberty and the pursuit of Happiness."

Drafting this declaration was arduous work for the Continental Congress. Heated debates resulted in eighty-six alterations of the document originally drafted by Thomas Jefferson. However, when it was finally published on July 4, 1776, everyone was aligned and the behavioral impact was instantaneous. Virtually overnight, it brought together the people of the thirteen colonies in a common cause to overcome enormous military and political challenges. More than two centuries after its composition, the Declaration of Independence towers as "the signal of arousing men to burst the chains . . . to assume the blessings and security of self-government" and to restore "the free right to the unbounded exercise of reason and freedom of opinion."

Once people understand the Guiding Precepts of an organization, they can begin to use them as day-to-day decision filters. The power of this should not be underestimated. Every day people are confronted with a multitude of decisions, large and small. Given the number of people making decisions in an organization, and the number of decisions each person must make each day, it is essential that there be a shared pattern of decision-making based on the Future Picture and the Guiding Precepts. Over time this pattern will be deeply ingrained. In short, the Guiding Precepts become "who we are."

THE TWO ELEMENTS OF A GUIDING PRECEPT

In the Prometheus Process, we've found it useful to define two levels of Guiding Precepts: Prime Directives and Rules of Engagement.

Guiding Precepts: Prime Directives

Prime Directives, the highest level of Guiding Precepts, are business or behavioral rules so important that their violation is absolutely intolerable.

Such was the Prime Directive created by Hippocrates, the celebrated Greek physician. The works attributed to him are the earliest extant Greek medical writings, and among them is the famous doctor's words that we now refer to as the Hippocratic oath. This fascinating code of ethics shows that in his time physicians were already organized into a guild, with regulations for training and a professional ideal that, with slight exceptions, remain relevant today.

One of the most widely known aspects of the Hippocratic oath is the injunction to the physician to do no harm: "I will prescribe regimens for the good of my patients according to my ability and my judgment and never do harm to anyone." Because the Hippocratic oath provides very specific behavioral boundaries, it has positively influenced the conduct of physicians for over two millennia.

Another example from Greek history is the harsh Prime Directive of the state of Sparta, where the warriors were told before they went into battle, "Come back carrying your shields or come back carried upon them." This meant no surrender and no running from a battle. Those who failed to honor this directive found themselves without a country.

The Ten Commandments provide such powerful Prime Directives that they have had an extraordinary influence on behavior for thousands of years.

Some modern business organizations are just as explicit in their Prime Directives—and with good reason. In the business world, Prime Directives are so fundamental that an employee either signs up and follows them, or doesn't belong in the organization.

The 3M Corporation encapsulated its intense commitment to innovation in its Prime Directive, "Thou shalt not kill a new product idea."

Many businesses and nonprofit organizations have non-negotiable rules that could be classified as Prime Directives. Airlines, for instance, teach their flight attendants that "Your primary concern is passenger safety."

The Prime Directives for Desert Storm were Grand Strategy ground rules making clear what was and was not permissible behavior; you may recall the rules from earlier in these pages:

- The war will be oriented against Saddam Hussein and his policies, not against the Iraqi people.
- We will keep Iraqi civilian casualties and property damage to an absolute minimum.
- We will keep American (and coalition) casualties to a minimum.
- The campaign will capitalize on American strengths and will avoid fighting the Iraqis on their terms.

These four Prime Directives provided a filter both for strategic planning and all of the subsequent tactical decisions, helping shape the outcome of Desert Storm.

What Prime Directives are appropriate for your organization? What rules need to be absolute? As you shape your Prime Directives, keep the following in mind:

- Make them few in number—ideally, no more than three or four.
- Choose them carefully. Never adopt a Prime Directive without fully thinking through the potential consequences.
- Once announced and distributed, take them seriously. Prime

Directives should never be optional. They are a prerequisite for participation in the organization.

If a rule is considered important, but violating it is not grounds for dismissal, then it does not rise to the level of a Prime Directive. It is something more temporary—a Rule of Engagement.

Guiding Precepts: Rules of Engagement

Like Prime Directives, Rules of Engagement are there to be followed, but they may change over time when circumstances warrant. Rules of Engagement are useful in establishing boundaries for behaviors and decisions within a specific operational context.

General Electric's policy of only staying in businesses in which it can be number one or number two in its market provides a good example of a business Rule of Engagement. With this standing rule in place, managers in a subsidiary like GE Capital know what is on the line if their company falls short of the standard. Likewise, no one in GE's mergers-and acquisitions department is likely to propose the acquisition of a company that is not first or second in its market, unless it could be brought up to that level very rapidly once acquired. In short, this Rule of Engagement is a very powerful tool with global impact on decisions within General Electric.

One of our clients, the Bama Companies, a major supplier to McDonald's, created a new mergers-and-acquisitions department as a part of their Future Picture. One of the Rules of Engagement they established for the new organization was that it would only acquire companies compatible with Bama's culture—a culture with an unusually high commitment to safety, integrity, and quality of life for all employees. As a result of this filter, decisions could be made quickly about what companies would even be considered. Bama believed that, as a result of this Guiding Precept, thousands of man-hours would be saved because no one would waste time researching or negotiating deals that would not be a good fit for their culture.

During a major change initiative, Motorola created a Rule of Engagement to address a pressing strategic concern: leadership assignments. Sandy Ogg, Corporate Vice President and Director of Motorola's Office of Leadership, explained in an interview with Leland:

> There was an urgent need for leadership flexibility. For example, if an opportunity or a crisis emerged in the handset business, we needed to be able to move our best talent there quickly.
>
> The problem with doing that was bureaucracy. You had to ask permission of the person's boss, who would inevitably say, "He's not ready," or "She's too important to our business," or "It would hurt us to lose him," or "I don't have a replacement." And that litany of excuses would kill the idea of moving someone, no matter how urgent or strategically important the move was to the company.
>
> I solved the problem by creating a Rule of Engagement relative to movement of leaders in Motorola. The rule is very simple: "Which issues are most critical to the company at this juncture? Who are the best leaders to address these issues?" Once we identified who those leaders were, they moved. Period. Only two people have veto power. One is the accepting manager, who has to agree that the person is right for the job. The other is the selected leader, who might have some legitimate personal reason not to move.
>
> Establishing that Rule of Engagement and enforcing it has made a huge difference to our success. Now, when someone tells me, "You're robbing Peter to pay Paul!" my response is, "Baloney. We're robbing Peter to win!"

Is it possible to achieve your Future Picture without having any ground rules? Sure, but at what cost? Bama could have achieved its Future Picture—to become a billion-dollar company—without stipulating the "cultural fit" requirement for acquisitions. In fact, it would have been far easier for it to find and acquire companies without this screen. But in the eyes of the Bama people, the cost would have been too great. So as a group, they made a conscious choice: "It is vitally important to us to arrive at our Future Picture with our culture intact."

Rules of Engagement should track and support the Future Picture. Assume, for example, that your company's Future Picture included a Key Descriptor that said, "We will be highly entrepreneurial." Entrepreneurs are generally thought of as people willing to take risks in the pursuit of significant gain. But how much risk is acceptable? Absent a Rule of Engagement that defines acceptable risk, people will waste time and money on products and projects that will never be approved.

Now suppose that your organization's leadership defined "being entrepreneurial" as open to exploring new opportunities, but with some definite limits on the level of risk they are willing to tolerate. In this case, an appropriate Rule of Engagement might be: "There will be no 'bet the company' projects and no projects that jeopardize a core part of the existing business." When this Rule of Engagement is clearly defined and communicated, people are far less likely to waste their time and everyone else's with ideas that might be good in themselves, but that don't pass muster with this particular decision filter. They are more likely to move faster because they can make decisions with the confidence that they are "doing the right thing" in the eyes of the organization.

MILITARY RULES OF ENGAGEMENT

The term "Rules of Engagement" derives from the military world, where it defines what is and is not permissible behavior in combat situations. These rules are not static; they are reconsidered as combat circumstances change.

During Desert Storm, the first F-15 fighters to sweep into Iraq had this Rule of Engagement: "If you see an airplane on radar or visually, shoot." Then, as the situation became more complex and more coalition planes hit the skies, this Rule of Engagement was tightened: "Do not shoot unless your electronic gear tells you that the target is an enemy." Still later in the war, when it became unlikely that any Iraqi aircraft were flying, the rule was tightened again to require positive visual identification.

The fact that the Rules of Engagement are not set in stone is a tremendous advantage. Few situations are static; when marketplace dynamics shift in a fundamental way or the organization moves into an entirely new situation, the Rules of Engagement should be reevaluated. Do yesterday's rules still make sense?

The task for leaders is to ensure that people have the right Rules of Engagement to meet the current situation, and that the rules are simple to understand. If they are too complex or too ambiguous, they are of little value. Most importantly, leaders must ensure that the *current* Rules of Engagement are known and under-stood throughout the organization.

There is one special benefit to the ability to redefine the Rules of Engagement: It helps you shift the organization's decision-making patterns. Used in this way, Rules of Engagement can be an antidote to "legacy" mind-sets and a powerful tool for managing *FastTime* structural change in an organization.

When shaping your Rules of Engagement, keep the following in mind:

- Rules of Engagement should be clear and straightforward—use the "keep it simple" principle.
- Rules of Engagements are not eternal. It is "how we do business now"—at a particular point in time. Be prepared to change the Rules of Engagement when circumstances warrant it.
- Until canceled or changed, each Rule of Engagement should be followed. Just because it is temporary does not mean it can be ignored.

HOW TO ENGRAVE THE GUIDING PRECEPTS

Merely defining your Guiding Precepts—the Prime Directives and Rules of Engagement—is not enough. It is essential to live them, and here is where the hard part begins. To understand the nature of the challenge, consider the dynamics between Calculated Rules and Axiomatic Behavior. Calculated Rules are what the person or company claims it is going to do. Axiomatic Behavior is what a person or a company does "when the chips are down."

Here is a simple example of the how the two play out. We're all familiar with what happens when a child wants a piece of candy before dinner. The Calculated Rule is, "No candy until after dinner." But typically, the child asks again and again until the parent is worn down and reverts to the Axiomatic Behavior, which is, "Just one piece!"

When push comes to shove, organizations, like families, often have difficulty sustaining their Calculated Rules. In a crunch, in a crisis, under pressure, the tendency is to revert to their Axiomatic Behavior, despite the many lofty pronouncements to the contrary. A classic example of this was IBM's new Rule of Engagement in the early 1980s: "Aggressively develop the personal computer market." The company followed this Calculated Rule for a while, but deeply ingrained in IBM's culture was another, more powerful Axiomatic Behavior based on a belief that "mainframes are our primary market."

A culture clash inevitably followed, pitting the iconoclastic "rogues" at the branch in Boca Raton, Florida (who were said to appear at work without the regulation gray suit!), and the corporate old guard at headquarters in Armonk, New York. Sad for IBM, the Axiomatic Behavior won the day. The personal computer people were pulled back to headquarters in Armonk, where there was ample supervision and stultification. Thereafter, IBM rapidly lost its extraordinary position in the PC world and went through ten nasty years of falling stock prices, falling market capitalization, and downsizing.

Unless you plan otherwise, Axiomatic Behaviors are likely to prevail in most organizations. To truly shape the behavioral patterns in an organization, the Guiding Precepts must be more than lofty pronouncements hung on the wall. They must be *engraved* into the organizational mind-set. How do you accomplish this?

First, include "as many people as you can stand" in defining them. Use Open Planning to ensure that the right choices are made and that—from day one—you are creating buy-in from a critical mass. Second, "walk the talk"—be consistent about adherence to the Guiding Precepts. They should become part of the organization's "genetic code."

People will move through some predictable phases on this journey. At first they will unconsciously violate the rules, simply because the expectations are new and unfamiliar. Then they will begin to notice themselves and others struggling with the ramifications of the precepts. At this stage, doubt may set in—"Can we really do this? Is it worth it?" Finally, if the leaders walk the talk and remain consistent, over time the Guiding Precepts will become part of the genetic code of the organization. This is the goal.

The process of engraving the Guiding Precepts can be assisted by:

- Developing the Guiding Precepts as part of the whole planning process with as many people involved as possible.
- Insisting, without exception, that senior managers make decisions and behave in accordance with the Guiding Precepts. (If there is a Precept they don't agree with, the organization should not adopt it to begin with.)
- Creating rewards and consequences associated with the Guiding Precepts.
- Continually reinforcing the Guiding Precepts, along with the Future Picture, in meetings, communications, and publications.
- Establishing a time frame for a behavioral transition—and being frank in acknowledging shortfalls and challenges during this period.

We've now covered three aspects of designing the future: Scoping the Environment, Painting the Future Picture, and Engraving the Guiding Precepts. In the next chapter, we will look at the last aspect: *establishing Measures of Merit.*

Chapter Debrief: Guiding Precepts

A Guiding Precept is a behavioral touchstone—a short statement about what is or what is not permissible behavior as people go about the work of achieving the Future Picture.

An effective Guiding Precept meets two conditions. First, it states, in the clearest possible terms, something that is considered to be of the highest philosophical or operational *importance.* Second, to the greatest extent possible, it is *differentiating.*

In the Prometheus Process, there are two levels of Guiding Precepts: Prime Directives and Rules of Engagement. Prime Directives—the highest level—are business or behavioral rules that are so important that their violation is absolutely intolerable. Rules of Engagement are useful in establishing boundaries for behaviors and decisions within a specific operational context.

Calculated Rules are what the person or company claims it intends to do. Axiomatic Behavior is what a person or a company actually does "when the chips are down."

Leaders must "walk the talk" until the Guiding Precepts become Axiomatic Behavior.

8

Measures of Merit

"You Get What You Measure."

Hannibal of Carthage is considered by many to be one of the greatest military leaders of all time. In 218 B.C., after Carthage lost command of the sea to Rome, Hannibal seized the initiative and invaded Italy by marching his army 1,500 miles overland from Spain across the Pyrenees, the south of France, and the Alps. Because of his brilliant orchestration of cavalry and infantry, as well as his innovative techniques in logistics, intelligence, and psychological warfare, he was the most formidable foe the Romans ever faced.

Hannibal's greatest victory came at the battle of Cannae, where the Romans attempted to destroy his army by directly attacking en masse with 80,000 men. Although the Romans had far superior numbers, Hannibal utterly defeated them with a tactical maneuver the Romans had never seen before—the refused center which led to a double envelopment. It was such a brilliant battle tactic that it is still being studied today. The encircling maneuver used by coalition forces in the Gulf War, with its left sweep to surround the Iraqi forces, bears a striking resemblance to the maneuver Hannibal introduced 2,200 years ago.

MEASURING STRATEGIC SUCCESS

Hannibal was certainly a tactical genius; but was he really a successful military leader? The answer depends on how you measure success. Hannibal succeeded in winning many battles on the Italian peninsula for over ten years. But winning battles is irrelevant unless they *enable you to realize your strategic objective*—your Future Picture.

The Carthaginians' Future Picture was a world in which they were free to conduct commerce, a world where the Romans did not dictate the rules. With that Future Picture, the success measure that really mattered was the destruction of Roman power, the epicenter of which was in the city of Rome itself.

After his annihilation of a great Roman army at Cannae, Hannibal refused to march on Rome, largely because he believed that the psychological impact of his victory would lead to a collapse of the Roman coalition against him. His second in command, Maharbal,

Battle of Cannae

First Phase

Second Phase

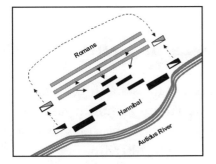 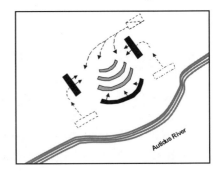

Figure 8.1 The Battle of Cannae

however, understood that strategic victory necessitated a march on Rome before the sun set on the battlefield. After failing to convince Hannibal, he is reported to have said in exasperation: "The gods rarely bestow all their gifts on a single man; on you, Hannibal, they have bestowed the gift of winning a battle, but they withheld the gift of winning a war."

One unarguable measure of strategic success is *whether you are better off after a campaign than you were before you began.* After Hannibal's ten-year campaign on the Italian peninsula, successful by most measures, the Carthaginians were on the verge of mortal peril.

The ultimate measure of success in war is winning the peace, not the battles. When you measure success at the strategic level, Hannibal failed miserably. What happened? After soundly defeating the Roman army at Cannae, Hannibal had a unique window of opportunity to achieve real success—strategic success. Rome lay undefended and, had he gone there, he could have destroyed the major Center of Gravity of his foe. Like so many others in war and business, however, he confused his tactical success with strategic success. Because he was winning battles, he thought he would win the war and the peace that would follow.

There's a powerful lesson in this story. *Tactical success does not equal strategic success.* The good leader never becomes mesmerized or overly impressed by tactical success. As strange as it seems, there is no absolute correlation between tactical success and strategic success. Recall that the North Vietnamese *lost* virtually every battle they fought against the Americans—yet won the war.

ESTABLISHING THE MEASURES OF MERIT

The final aspect in Designing the Future is to establish the strategic Measures of Merit that will make the Future Picture measurable, and that will provide understandable strategic measures through which all tactical events and decisions can be filtered.

If you fail to spend adequate time and energy on this step at each level of your organization, you may end up like Hannibal.

Remember that tactical success—winning battles—does not equal strategic success—winning the war.

How can you tell the difference between tactical success and strategic success? Consider the impact of an event on your Future Picture. Given the Carthaginians' Future Picture (a world free of Roman domination and interference), winning the battle of Cannae meant nothing in itself. What really mattered was overthrowing the power of the Roman Empire.

MEASURE ENDS, NOT MEANS

Like a compelling destination (Future Picture) and clear-cut ground rules (Guiding Precepts), Measures of Merit are intended to *drive strategic thinking and behavior*—the ideas and actions necessary to win long-term. Again we ask the question, how do we tell the difference between strategic measures—Measures of Merit—and measures that were only on a tactical level? Tactical measures evaluate the quality or quantity of tactical activities (the means) as almost an end unto themselves. Measures of Merit evaluate results against Future Picture objectives (the ends).

Higher-level measures are not always obvious. Consider what happened when the United States began the Lend Lease program to support the British in their effort against Germany during World War II. The Germans, of course, attacked the merchant ships carrying war matériel to England (unarmed, because the United States was officially still a "neutral"). German submarines and, more dangerously, German long-range bombers began to have a devastating impact. Something had to be done, so the United States Navy installed antiaircraft guns on the merchant ships and manned them with trained Navy gunners.

After the Japanese attack on Pearl Harbor, the Navy ordered the guns and crews off the merchant vessels for immediate service in the Pacific theater. When the inevitable protest arose, the Navy explained its rationale: In the time the guns and crews had been on the merchant ships, they had failed to shoot down any significant number of German bombers. By this tactical measure, the effort was a complete waste of scarce resources vitally needed to stop the onrushing Japanese.

Fortunately, cooler heads intervened before the deed was done and asked the important question: What was the strategic purpose of putting the guns on the ships in the first place? Was it to shoot down German planes?

Obviously the strategic purpose of the guns was to improve the odds of the merchant ships and their cargo making it safely to England. Since installation of the guns, the number of merchant ships sunk by German bombers had fallen significantly.

If the gunners weren't shooting down bombers, why had the number of ships sunk by aircraft gone down so much? Answer: When the merchant ships were unarmed, the German pilots could fly in almost at masthead level. At that height there was a very high probability of hitting the ship with a bomb or torpedo. Once the antiaircraft gunners began firing at them, however, and they faced a stream of tracers, the masthead flight path didn't seem like such a good idea. The German pilots did what any smart pilot would do: attack from a higher, safer altitude. Unfortunately for the Germans, bombs or torpedoes dropped from a higher altitude were significantly less likely to hit their target. Ergo, few ships sunk.

Once the effectiveness of antiaircraft guns was measured strategically, the decision to remove the guns was reversed. The guns stayed on the ships—with one minor modification. The Navy gunners went to the Pacific, where they were urgently needed, and merchant sailors took over the duty of manning the guns. The fact that they were untrained wasn't a barrier . . . since it didn't really matter whether or not they hit anything.

THE NORM: TACTICAL MEASURES

Most organizations tend to rely solely on tactical measures. What are called "high-level measures" are simply an aggregate of all of the tactical measures. For example, until fairly recently the United States

Air Force assessed a day's combat operations by counting the number of aircraft flown, the tons of bombs dropped, the number of targets hit, and the amount of fuel consumed. Those statistics may have been useful and necessary. They did not, however, provide any information relevant to strategic results. The key question—"What was the actual effect on the opponent?"—was not being addressed.

In the mid-1990s the North America Marketing and Refining Group of Mobil Oil (now ExxonMobil) discovered just what happens when an organization focuses on tactical measures. "Many of the measures we had historically employed drove people to behavior that didn't get us where we wanted to be," remembers company executive Brian Baker. Behaviors were short-term and silocentric, or localized within a department. The collective result of this behavior put the group at the bottom of its industry ranking. In charge of a massive turnaround, Baker linked everyone's performance measures to the overall strategy. In two years flat, the company went from the bottom to the top of the rankings.

One large, hierarchical medical center learned the hard way just how counterproductive stand-alone tactical measures can be. Like many health-care organizations, it tried to reduce financial shortfalls through cost-cutting. Every department in the medical center was required to "share the pain," and department managers were told to promptly reduce expenses by a designated percentage. Stovepipe budgeting left no room for coordination across departments and no reward for collaboration.

Under intense pressure to reach the tactical cost target by which they would be measured, the managers of the radiology department came up with a way to cut costs: Make only one copy of an X ray and keep it in a central location. This immediately lowered expenses in the radiology department, but it disrupted the entire medical center and actually increased its overall costs. In the old process, when doctors ordered X rays, copies of the film were delivered to them. In the new process, highly paid doctors, under enormous time constraints, had to go to the central repository to review the X rays. Needless to say, the doctors were furious and the efficiency of the facility deteriorated.

You get what you measure. If you use stand-alone, tactical measures, don't be surprised by the stand-alone tactical behavior that follows. The radiology department was given a single, absolute tactical measure. It optimized its own costs, ignoring a collective impact that was bad for the overall system.

Think about the measures that the people in your organization track. How many of those evaluate tactical "means"—the equivalent of bombs dropped, fuel consumed, percentages of potential targets hit? In the business world, most managers are focused on this kind of tactical measurement—sales calls made, efficiency of service, cost per unit, and so on. Regardless of the value in tracking such statistics, remember that the greater significance lies in measures that track actual progress toward the ends.

STRATEGIC PERSPECTIVE

There was a six-year-old girl whose older brother thought she was a dimwit because every time he gave her the choice between a dime and dollar, she chose the dime. He thought this was so hilarious that whenever his friends were around, he entertained them by offering his younger sister the dime-or-dollar choice over and over.

But the six-year-old had a long-term success strategy: Collect as many dimes as she could get. As long as she never chose the dollar, her brother kept giving her the dimes.

When you measure strategically on a regular basis, your mind-set changes. Your time horizon expands as you begin to consider long-term results and the cumulative effects of a succession of events.

Many people, however, find it extremely difficult to mentally climb "out of the weeds" and see the Big Picture. A good example of this kind of tactical mentality occurred during the Desert Storm air campaign. One of the key objectives was to "turn off" the electricity in Baghdad and other areas of Iraq as quickly as possibly. Through the courtesy of real-time feedback from CNN, supported by other intelligence information, it appeared that the desired result—to disable Iraq's electrical system—had been rapidly achieved. But not everyone in the Washington bureaucracy was measuring the air campaign results strategically or systemically.

About ten days into the war, John Warden happened to read an intelligence report done by the Defense Intelligence Agency that had been circulated in the White House and elsewhere in Washington. In essence, it said that the campaign against the electrical facilities had been a failure. John asked one of his associates to call the analyst who had written the report and ask him to explain his strange conclusion. The conversation that followed illustrates the nature of a tactical mind-set. John recalls:

> The analyst got a little bit huffy when he was questioned about the rationale behind his report. "Let us say that there are about two hundred electrical targets in Iraq," he said, "and that you had only hit about twenty of them. That's only ten percent effectiveness after ten days. In my mind, that's a failure!"
>
> When asked if he had been watching television the night the war began and had seen the lights go out in Baghdad, he responded, "Sure."
>
> And had he seen lights on anyplace else in Iraq? No, he hadn't. He was then asked, "Doesn't the fact that all the lights were out probably mean that the campaign against electricity was close to being one hundred percent successful?"
>
> He countered, "That conclusion is ridiculous. Do the math. Two hundred targets! Twenty hit. That's ten percent and that equals failure! Goodbye!"

This analyst had a tactical mind-set, and so was measuring the air campaign results at the tactical level. Moreover, he was not considering the systemic effect on the opponent. Strategically, it didn't matter one iota how many facilities you hit, or how many you did not hit. What mattered was whether or not the desired *system effect* was achieved.

And it was.

The desired system effect was "no electricity." And the less effort required to accomplish that systems effect, the better.

EVALUATING EVENTS STRATEGICALLY

When you have a strategic perspective, you evaluate the success of your "battles" in the context of your strategic objectives. You also tend to judge tactical successes and tactical setbacks through a strategic lens: "What is the long-term strategic impact of this event?" Unlike Hannibal, you don't confuse temporary tactical success with long-term strategic success. By the same token, you don't interpret temporary tactical setbacks as strategic failure. In fact, you look for strategic opportunities in tactical setbacks.

Early in its history, Southwest Airlines turned a difficult tactical setback into an opportunity. In 1973, Braniff was trying to put Southwest out of business by slashing its fares to $13 between Dallas and Houston. It was only the second year of operations for Southwest and the fledgling airline was still not turning a profit. Dallas–Houston was its only moneymaking route, and to make matters worse, the airline was dangerously low on cash at the time—a fact of which Braniff was well aware.

Braniff thought it had struck a lethal blow that would bankrupt its start-up rival, but Southwest turned the tables. Rather than responding directly and tactically, it used the attack as an opportunity to establish its strategic low-fare brand image with Texans and simultaneously catapult itself into profitability. The CEO decided to snatch victory from the jaws of defeat with an innovative, two-pronged approach.

First, to build its image and market share, Southwest bought a multi-page newspaper ad to explain the David-and-Goliath nature of its fare war with Braniff, with the deucedly clever headline, "NOBODY'S GOING TO SHOOT SOUTHWEST AIRLINES OUT OF THE SKY FOR A LOUSY $13."

That captured the attention of the Texas media and the imagination of many potential passengers. On top of that, to maintain its cash flow, Southwest wasn't going along with the price cut just to remain competitive. But to encourage passengers to pay its higher fare (not *that* much higher—still only $26), the company offered a free fifth of scotch, whiskey, or vodka with the ticket. This made travelers *very* happy, and the airline sold enough tickets to quickly solve its cash crunch. Newspapers would soon report that the promotion had made Southwest Airlines, at least for a short time, "the largest distributor of Chivas, Crown Royal and Smirnoff in the state of Texas!" Here we see a tactical battle won that added power to the Southwest strategic objective.

BUILDING STRATEGIC MEASURES

How do you build a strategic perspective into every level of your organization? Here are three suggestions:

- Define and establish your strategic Measures of Merit and communicate them to everyone in the organization.
- Make sure that people understand the core concept: Tactical success is important, but the ultimate strategic goal is the measure of true success—*"Go to Rome."*
- Create an integrated measuring system that links day-to-day performance to strategic Measures of Merit on a consistent and continuous basis. If a tactical action doesn't support a strategic objective, it probably shouldn't be done—and, in any event, should not be a source of reward. Recognize tactical effort, reward strategic success.

Just as no Key Descriptor in your Future Picture is more important than another—together, they are brush strokes that make a whole canvas—no Measure of Merit is more important than another. Some will seem more important than others. But all are important to gauging success.

Why does this matter? It's not uncommon for an organization to become overly focused on a single measure, to its detriment. In early 1993, Dell Computer was on the brink of disaster owing to a strategy focused exclusively on growth. Mesmerized by this one measure, the leadership faced a series of compounding problems: Profits and liquidity disappeared; there was insufficient working capital to invest in new technologies; the stock price was down.

In 1993 CEO Michael Dell realized that his company was in serious trouble despite its apparent success. It hit him that his preoccupation with growth was the problem: It was driving decisions at all levels that could shortly lead to disaster. He quickly rebalanced his strategic measurement to: "liquidity, profitability, and growth—in that order." In his book, *Direct from Dell,* Dell describes the impact:

> Once we established clear metrics and measurements, it was easy to see which businesses were performing or not and to change strategy accordingly. For example, we changed our information systems so that a sales person could see the level of margin for a product literally as he or she was selling it on the phone. Previously, you might have had a case where two sales people would each sell $1 million worth of our products, but one might have a 28 percent profit margin and the other only 8 percent.

Dell's compensation system changed from an emphasis on top-line sales to a more sophisticated measure of profitability, motivating people to ensure that each sale achieved the goal.

In sum, making everyone aware of the strategic Measures of Merit—all of them—is a powerful tool to promote thinking and behavior that directly support the Future Picture and related strategy.

USING EXTERNAL MEASURES

A strategic Measure of Merit should be as objective as possible. The most objective measures are those that are external—measures that come from outside the organization.

For example, an organization's stock price compared to many other company stock prices will show how impartial observers are rating the company's future (with the assumption that the stock market is always reflecting a view about tomorrow). Figure 8.2 shows the price of a company's stock against Standard & Poor's 500 Index. This comparison clearly says that the market is valuing this company's stock at something less than the average stock component of the S&P 500. This company might think itself to be the best

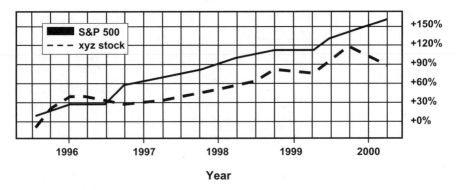

Figure 8.2 External Measures

in its market, but the comparison is of little interest to investors in general, who will normally look for a stock that will give them at least average returns.

Another way to ensure objectivity is to measure outside your own industry. Compare your results in specific performance areas against the best-in-class companies in the world, even if those companies are in other industries.

Why should you be concerned about what companies in other industries are doing? After all, you aren't competing with them. Well, the fact that you compare favorably to others in your own industry may make you feel good, but it's not really relevant if your industry overall measures poorly against the best-in-class.

The fact is, whenever you lag behind *anyone* in performance, that lag is pointed out as an opportunity gap. Let's look at a practical example.

The curve illustrated in Figure 8.3 shows an estimate of technological progress for the U.S. Defense Department. It is impressive when compared to any other country's military. However, compared to the technical progress of the integrated circuit industry after 1975, the Defense Department's technological progress does not look so good!

In the Information Age, the march toward excellence knows no boundaries. When something is being done exceptionally well in one industry, aggressive competitors in other industries will notice and use it, assuming they see an opportunity for a competitive

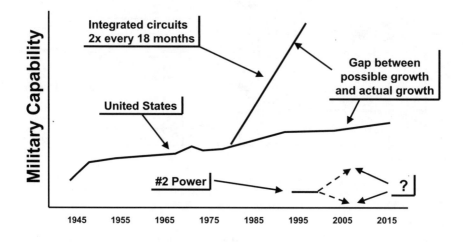

Figure 8.3 The Dangers of Self-Measurement

advantage. This is what happened with the quality movement, which was pioneered by Xerox but quickly spread to other competitors and to other industries.

DEVELOPING YOUR MEASURES OF MERIT

How can you develop Measures of Merit for your organization? Begin your measurement system from the highest level, the Future Picture. Once you've defined a Measure of Merit for each of the twelve Key Descriptors of the Future Picture, you will have a balanced, strategic set of measures with which to assess your progress—and a superb tool to use as a decision filter at all levels. Then, reassess all your current measures at lower echelons of the organization to be sure they are in alignment.

Below is an example of the Measures of Merit for our fictitious public company, the FastWin Corporation, first introduced in the Future Picture chapter.

2005 FUTURE PICTURE FOR FASTWIN CORPORATION
KEY DESCRIPTORS AND MEASURES OF MERIT

FINANCIAL POSITION

Key Descriptor:

FastWin will have a market capitalization twice its current size, and remuneration of employees will have increased in direct proportion to the successful achievement of this financial position.

Measure of Merit:

FastWin's stock price has risen appropriately and employee compensation has risen commensurately.

MARKET POSITION

Key Descriptor:

FastWin will be a market driver and leader.

Measure of Merit:

The rest of the market is madly copying FastWin's leads; FastWin never finds itself in the position of having to react to a competitor.

BUSINESS AREAS

Key Descriptor:

FastWin will continue to manufacture and market high-margin medical devices for professional caregivers. It also will explore opportunities in the self-care medical market.

Measure of Merit:

90% of FastWin net revenues are derived from high-margin medical devices. FastWin has at least one product generating significant profit in the self-care market.

INNOVATION

Key Descriptor:

FastWin continues to innovate in technology, business processes, and medical products and services that will have quantum effects on business results at every level.

Measure of Merit:

30% of revenue each year comes from products and services introduced or updated during the previous year.

STAKEHOLDER PERCEPTION

Key Descriptor:

FastWin's stakeholders will see the organization as a smart place to invest their time, energy, and money.

Measure of Merit:

Overall stakeholder-satisfaction survey results are at 90% or above.

OUTSIDER PERCEPTION

Key Descriptor:

FastWin will have a reputation as a solid financial performer that offers high-quality, leading-edge products.

Measure of Merit:

FastWin's stock carries at least a 20% higher multiple than others in the same market space (and has appreciated per the Measure under Financial Position). Independent reviewers consistently cite the value and quality of the company's products.

WORKFORCE CHARACTERISTICS

Key Descriptor:

FastWin will have a highly productive, entrepreneurial workforce.

Measure of Merit:

FastWin's profit per employee has doubled over 36 months, which equates to about a 25% per annum growth rate. Employees come up with new ideas and processes at every level of the company.

BRAND

Key Descriptor:	Measure of Merit:
The FastWin brand will be the gold standard in the medical device industry.	FastWin's margins are the highest in the industry.

CORPORATE CULTURE

Key Descriptor:	Measure of Merit:
FastWin will have an open culture that encourages smart risk-taking.	Doors are open, campaign rooms are in use, everyone knows the game plans, junior employees regularly challenge senior executives, and honest failures are applauded.

CORPORATE CITIZENSHIP

Key Descriptor:	Measure of Merit:
FastWin will help select communities acquire the latest medical technology.	More than one community has equipment it otherwise would not have had, and community leaders are vociferous in their thanks.

OWNERSHIP

Key Descriptor:	Measure of Merit:
FastWin will remain a public company with substantial stock ownership by its employees.	Most employees own stock, and options have become a major part of compensation.

INCENTIVE PHILOSOPHY

Key Descriptor:

FastWin will reward results, recognize activity, and make many of its employees rich.

Measure of Merit:

25% of employee compensation is bonus (cash and/or equity like stock, options, etc.) based on performance of the company, team, and individual employees as thanks for hard work (effort); and average employee net worth attributable to FastWin has gone up proportional to company appreciation.

When the Measures of Merit are established, you've completed the first imperative of the Prometheus Process—*Design the Future.* Now you are ready to address the next imperative: *Target for Success*

Chapter Debrief: Measures of Merit

Measures of Merit evaluate results against the ends—the Future Picture. Tactical measures evaluate the quality or quantity of tactical activities—the means—as almost an end unto themselves.

You get what you measure. Measures of Merit drive strategic thinking and behavior. If you use stand-alone, tactical measures, don't be surprised by the stand-alone tactical behavior that follows.

When you measure strategically on a regular basis, your mind-set changes. Your time horizon expands as you begin to consider long-term results and the cumulative effects of a succession of events. Don't confuse temporary tactical success with long-term strategic success. By the same token, don't interpret temporary tactical setbacks as strategic failure. Look for strategic opportunities in tactical setbacks.

Create an integrated measuring system that links day-to-day performance to strategic Measures of Merit on a consistent and continuous basis.

A strategic Measure of Merit should be as objective as possible. The most objective measures are those that are external—measures that come from outside the organization.

PROMETHEUS PROCESS

IMPERATIVE TWO

TARGET FOR SUCCESS

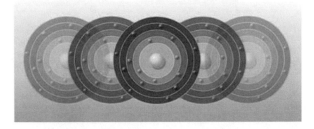

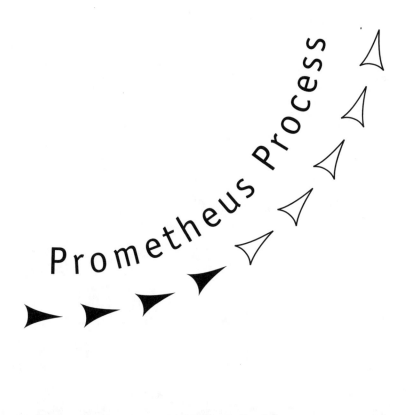

9

The Five Rings

"The most extraordinary effort is pointless
if it is not focused on the right targets."

In planning the Desert Storm air campaign, the system mind-set
was the real differentiator, the "magic" that ultimately led to such a
rapid, decisive victory. That mind-set is based on some fundamental assumptions about changing systems.

Remember the Promethic Laws: "All systems have Centers of
Gravity and the systems change when their Centers of Gravity
change." How do you apply this to strategy? Target your efforts
where you can have disproportionate impact—the Centers of Gravity in the system. Hit these Centers of Gravity and you will see
rapid, and potentially permanent, change in the system you're
attacking. Hit the majority of targets that are *not* Centers of Gravity,
and the system will shrug off your efforts.

Again from the Promethic Laws: "The extent and probability of
system change is directly proportional to the number of Centers of
Gravity affected and the speed at which they are affected." Systems
have inertia and resist change. If we affect Centers of Gravity

slowly, the system quickly "learns" how to repair itself, whereas rapid impact on Centers of Gravity significantly reduces the system's ability to learn or to react.

TARGETING CENTERS OF GRAVITY

In our work with numerous organizations, we have found that most people, leaders included, at first have difficulty with the concept of Centers of Gravity as targets. That's understandable because it is a very different way of thinking. People are accustomed to organization audits, from/to charts, and leader-defined initiatives. Invariably, people ask, "What does (the leader) want us to do?" When that question is answered, they want to move immediately into task definition—the how-to: generating action ideas, energetically debating them, and then winnowing the list down to some priority action items.

Diving down into the task level at this point is a major mistake. It is a classic case of getting the proverbial "cart before the horse." The "cart," in this instance, is the how-to. The "horse" is the system target you're aiming at. In short, before task lists are created, everyone needs to understand which targets they are to hit. In other words, it's important to identify the Centers of Gravity against which scarce resources will be directed.

There are usually multiple Centers of Gravity, all of which are interrelated. Some of them may have more influence on achieving the Future Picture than others. For example, you may need the support of an influential executive or leadership group that exerts a disproportionate influence on the system. You might also need to change a key organizational process like marketing, R&D, or internal communications.

Once you have identified the system's potential leverage points, you'll next address some key questions about them. Which are the high-leverage targets? What are the desired effects, the intended outcomes, for each? Until you know the answers, don't dive down to the task level. If you don't know what you're trying to accomplish, generating action agendas is not only premature, it is a colossal waste of time.

Selecting the right strategic targets is critical to winning in *FastTime*. If you don't get the strategic targets right, it will be difficult, if not impossible, to change the system. Failure to define the high-leverage system targets and the desired effects during the planning phase leads to less than optimum results in the execution phase. At the end of the day, everyone could end up having worked very hard but accomplishing very little simply because their efforts were aimed at the wrong targets.

What is the leader's role in system targeting? More important than anything else is to ensure that everyone focuses on identifying the Centers of Gravity as the first order of business after designing the future. The temptation, as we've pointed out, will be to "get down to business" and bypass the target selection phase. This is the natural tendency of action-oriented people, who will always want to begin working as soon as possible to "make things happen." Unfortunately, the things that are happening might not be the right ones from a systemic standpoint. To have a systemic impact, the right targets must be selected and they must be attacked in parallel—many must be affected with as much simultaneity as possible. This is how you increase your probability of success.

THE FIVE RINGS MODEL

Centers of Gravity can seem like an abstraction, so it is helpful to have a visual model to give you a comprehensible picture of a complex phenomenon, and to help you prioritize your attack plan.

The Five Rings model (Figure 9.1) was developed by John Warden and during the planning of Desert Storm, became the primary tool for understanding Iraq as a system and for identifying its Centers of Gravity. Since 1995, this same model has been successfully applied to planning challenges within a variety of industries, including high-tech, entertainment, finance, health care, and food service.

The Five Rings model makes systems thinking usable in the real world. It makes clear that *all* systems have similar kinds of components and are susceptible to very similar analysis. The model presents in visual form the five categories of system components common to all dynamic systems.

- Every system has *Leadership* components that give it direction and help it respond to changes in its external and internal environments (Ring 1, the center of the system).
- Every system has *Processes* that convert energy from one form to another and enable the components of the system to interact (Ring 2).
- Every system has a visible or invisible *Infrastructure* that holds the components together (Ring 3).
- Every system has a general *Population* of similar groups—normally people (Ring 4).
- Every system has *Agents* that exert power to sustain, advance, and protect the system (Ring 5).

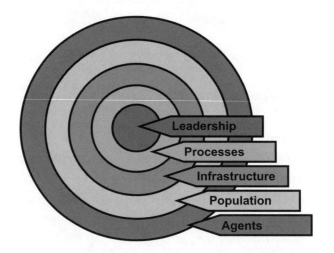

Figure 9.1 The Five Rings

Each of the rings will contain one or more Centers of Gravity that will have a significant impact on the entire system if they are altered in any way. The visual depiction of the Five Rings helps us remember that we are always working with a whole system and that our objective is always to force the whole system to change in the way we want it to change.

The Five Rings graphic also begins to give us some ideas of relative importance. In some cases, we might be able to induce a system to change adequately by doing the right thing to the Leadership ring.

Suppose you want to sell a radical product to a very large company. You could make a sales call on just the Chief Executive Officer of the company and you might have a sale. But call on a Junior Purchasing Agent in a fifth-ring Purchasing Department, and your chances of closing the sale will be slim at best—you'll probably have to present your product again and again. Now think for a moment about relative expenditures of energy: One key call takes less time and less effort.

A reasonable objection at this point is that you cannot get to the CEO to make the sales call. Paula Marshall-Chapman of the Bama Companies tells the story of how her father cornered Ray Kroc, founder of McDonald's—clearly a Leadership Center of Gravity—to insist that Kroc personally try Bama's new one-portion pie.

Kroc, who previously had refused to consider desserts in the young McDonald's, loved the pie and subsequently gave Bama the order. No amount of talking to anyone else in the McDonald's organization could have produced this result.

If you can identify a Center of Gravity, you can find a way to affect it. In the Ray Kroc case, a daring but small energy investment led to a major sale. In general, doing things to Centers of Gravity toward the middle of the Five Rings will have more impact than doing something to a Center of Gravity on the periphery.

Remember, though, that systems resist change. Bypassing that purchasing clerk can sometimes cause real problems. So plan for it. The best approach will always consider the *whole* system and use *across-the-board* impact to get the job done—and keep it done.

THE FIVE RINGS MODEL: A UNIVERSAL TOOL

What could drug enforcement agencies in Kansas, New York, and Alabama, a video game designer in Hollywood, and a food company in Oklahoma possibly have in common? All of them have successfully applied the same planning tool—the Five Rings Model—to develop a *systems strategy.*

When a drug-enforcement task force in Montgomery, Alabama, wanted to dismantle a drug-trafficking organization, it used the Five Rings Model to help all of the agents get a clear picture of the overall system. In the first of the five rings, *Leadership,* they identified the people whose arrests would potentially cause the drug operation to collapse. They then identified high-leverage targets in each of the other four rings: *Processes,* which included drug production and money laundering; *Infrastructure,* such as planes, boats, and trucks for transport, stash sites, and communication equipment; *Population,* like suppliers, dealers, chemists, and pilots; and *Agents* like surveillance and security people. Once they had identified these Centers of Gravity and defined the desired effects, they concentrated their resources on the most crucial targets.

Says Jason Amoriell, the intelligence expert who instructed the task force in the use of the Five Rings, "Sometimes an investigation becomes reactive, frustrating the police. Arrest a guy one day, and the next day, new agents are selling drugs on the street again." When Amoriell introduced the Five Rings to agencies like the Kansas City Drug Enforcement Agency, the New York Police Department, and the Montgomery, Alabama, task force, they all quickly learned to focus their efforts on the targets that could collapse an entire drug-trafficking *system.*

At the other end of the reality spectrum, television writer and video-game designer Flint Dille used the Five Rings model to create a system composed of characters and game scenarios. The system was Soviet Strike, a video game that went platinum after its release by Electronic Arts. Without the holistic perspective provided by the Five Rings model, says Dille, the game wouldn't have been as comprehensive or exciting:

We started with the *Leadership* ring. About the bad guys, we'd say "Who are the leaders?" Then we asked, "What are the key *Processes* we need to design into the game?" We looked at the *Infrastructure* ring and asked, "Where are the depots, bridges, and headquarters?"

Then we thought about the *Population* that we wanted to inhabit this virtual world. "How many good guys, bad guys, and regular people?" And last, but not least, "How will we design our *Agents*? What do they look like? How will they compete?"

Flint Dille also used the Five Rings to design a hierarchy of monsters for his game T.R.A.X., which was named Party Game of the Year in 1995 by the *Chicago Sun-Times* and optioned by the Fox television network. "The Five Rings apply to any creative undertaking," he says.

Texas Instruments' leaders used the Five Rings model to find the key leverage points in the semiconductor industry. McDonald's corporate staff, suppliers, and franchisees used it to map their national supply chain system, and then map the system within an individual store. Many other organizations in a variety of industries—entertainment, finance, health care, construction, and food service, to name a few—have employed it with equal success.

When John Warden and his Checkmate team first used the Five Rings on a large scale for a major crisis, it was to meet the urgent need for a decisive air campaign. They were not thinking about the impact it might ultimately have in fields well beyond the geopolitical one for which John had designed it.

Since Desert Storm, many Air Force and other military professionals both in the U.S. and around the world have embraced the Five Rings approach to systems planning. Numerous books and articles have been written about it in the military press. Given the extraordinary success of the Desert Storm air campaign, none of this is particularly surprising. What *is* surprising, however, is how effectively and broadly the Five Rings model has been applied in the nonmilitary world.

The Five Rings model is universally applicable because it provides a simple and reliable way to visualize any system. The model allows a large group of people to build a shared understanding of the key components in the system they need to change. And because it provides a common language, it also improves the group's ability to discuss complex systems issues.

Most important, the normal inclination to treat symptoms, rather than root causes, goes by the wayside because a critical mass of people begins to see the system dynamics in a tangible way. They tend to conclude that the best ways to solve problems and realize opportunities are not necessarily the most obvious "single-point" ways.

THE FIVE RINGS MODEL IN PRACTICE

To better understand the Five Rings model, let's examine its application to four different systems—the human body, the nation-state, a business organization, and a market.

Ring 1: LEADERSHIP / components that set direction for the system

- In the *human body,* the brain is the primary leadership component because it directs the rest of the body.
- The Leadership ring of the *nation-state* certainly includes the most senior official like a president or prime minister. However, there are many others who affect the direction of the system. For instance, the leadership of the United States includes not only the President, but also other groups and institutions like the media, the Congress, financial powers, and the courts. Their respective decisions and actions give direction to the country.
- The Leadership ring of a *business organization* contains the individuals (or in some cases the hierarchical units) that give direction to a company. In most cases, the obvious people like the Chief Executive Officer and Chief Operating Officer will fall in this category, but it would be a major error to include only the officially designated company leaders. We would expect to see

included in this ring some informal leaders and some major influencers who are not even in the company.

- The Leadership ring of a *market* system contains the organizations and individuals that give direction to the market. This includes the market-leading companies, the market-leading customers and suppliers, the market-leading financial institutions, the political leaders who do (or could) affect the market positively or negatively, and the primary media that report on the market. To move a market, you must affect many of these leadership elements in a reasonably short period of time.

A key assumption in the Five rings model is that the Leadership ring exercises a disproportionate influence on the system. Because the Centers of Gravity identified in the Leadership ring are in a position to help or hinder almost without limit, it's of the highest importance to spend whatever time is necessary to identify these people or institutions and to spend the energy to affect them.

Ring 2: PROCESSES / components that convert energy within the system

- In the *human body,* the circulatory system converts oxygen and food into energy used by the rest of the body.
- In the *nation-state,* there are key energy-conversion processes like communications (which convert something expressed in one place to be perceived in another part of the system and which allow the parts of the system to talk to each other); agriculture (in which the energy of human labor and machines converts plants and animals into foods for the table); and electricity generation (in which energy from fuel or water power is converted into a form that drives our computers and lights our homes). Without such processes, the nation-state system soon falls into disarray.
- The Processes ring in a *business organization* covers those processes within a company that convert ideas, money, or material into components necessary for the company to function and to have salable products.

- The Processes ring in a *market* contains those elements that allow the market to function—processes involving market communication, idea development, commercialization, selling, production, and staffing, to name a few. To have a major impact on a market, you will normally need to affect one or more of these processes in such a way that your organization benefits from the change.

As you look at the key Process ring components, you might be inclined to see them as depictions of your current organizational structure or as potential organizing ideas. Don't automatically assume, however, that what you're currently doing is what you *should* be doing in the process area. To achieve your Future Picture, some processes may need to improve and new ones may need to be developed.

Ring 3: INFRASTRUCTURE / components that hold the system together

- In the *human body,* the connective tissue (tendons, ligaments, etc.) and skin constitute the system infrastructure that holds the bones in place and gives the body its shape.
- In the *nation-state,* the infrastructure consists of highways, railroads, airports, canals, and a variety of other visible, physical things.
- The Infrastructure ring for an *organization* and a *market* includes things that bind the entity together—physical things like computer networks and telephone systems, as well as nonphysical elements such as hierarchy rules, business models, and protocols.

Notice that the components of the Infrastructure ring are relatively static and normally do not change very quickly. They may exist for reasons that have nothing to do with the company or market. Of course, infrastructure components can and do change over time, but at any given moment (which may extend far into the future), they are fixed and not subject to rapid alteration.

Ring 4: **POPULATION/components that can be classified by function**

- In the *human body,* one example of "population" is the various kinds of cells—skin cells, bone cells, nerve cells, and the like.
- In the *nation-state,* the population consists of various demographic groups, each of which has certain shared attributes and preferences. There are a variety of classifications, including gender, ethnicity, educational level, economic status, professional affiliation, and so on.
- The Population ring within an *organization* contains the groupings—the demographics—of its people. These are not specific people, but are *categories* of people who have enough similarity that you can communicate with them and affect them to some extent as a group. For example, you could seek to affect all engineers versus Bob Smith, an individual in the engineering department.
- The Population ring within a *market* contains the groupings of people who constitute the market. Knowing the groups of people in the market gives you the ability to affect the market via the Population ring Centers of Gravity without having to deal with each of the individuals.

Obviously, you can be much more precise and effective when you deal with people as individuals. In the real world, however, especially in larger organizations, this can be difficult and very slow. If we reach individuals through their groups we can accelerate the effect, and in some instances actually improve the likelihood that a message will be accepted by a critical mass.

Although the Population ring will rarely be decisive by itself in moving us toward our Future Picture, when approached creatively it can play a very significant role. Consider this example:

An overseas company wanted to sell its soft drinks to big U.S. grocery chains. It had no luck in acquiring shelf space through conventional channels, nor did it succeed with direct approaches to senior management.

It decided, then, to focus on the employees of a chain that had an employee profit-sharing plan. The soft-drink company held parking-lot meetings and used targeted advertising to make the point that its beverages had a higher profit margin than Coke or Pepsi.

After a short time, the chain's rank and file began badgering management about the product. To appease them, management finally agreed to provide shelf space for the beverages—which turned out to be quite successful. In this instance, a creative approach to the Population ring paid off handsomely.

Ring 5: AGENTS / components that actively promote and defend the system

- In the *human body,* there are groups of cells that become potent agents in defending the system against disease. For example, some leukocytes take on invading germs, while others make the blood clot in response to a wound.
- In the *nation-state,* the agents would include the military and police, as well as the various government agencies that are chartered to either promote or defend the agenda of the system.
- The Agents ring in an *organization* or *market* contains the units within (and in some cases outside) the system that are responsible for taking action—selling, buying, protecting, advertising, and so on. These organizational units, like a country's military or police, act on behalf of the organization but do not (or at least should not) establish policy.

Because agents do not make policy, components in the Agents ring should not command too much of our attention. This is not to say that you don't need to deal with them; it simply means that an equivalent amount of energy expended to change inner rings will likely have more effect.

Another way to think about the fifth ring is that it's the realm of tactics. Consider, for instance, the agents in a low-end retail store: salespeople. Suppose the goal was to double profits and, to accomplish that, you instituted an intensive customer-service training program for all clerks. Now assume that, as a result of that program, the salespeople become twice as good at customer service. What effect would that have on profits, and how quickly?

The chances that this store will double its profits from that effort alone would be quite small. In addition, if the company has many stores, the energy required to find and train good salespeople would be enormous and quite expensive.

What if the same amount of energy was focused instead on affecting components in one of the inner rings? For instance, focusing in the Processes ring on improving the selection and pricing processes could yield a significant payoff across all stores. If properly done, these process improvements could improve profitability in most stores even in the absence of superb salespeople.

The bottom line is this: Concentrating efforts on the fifth ring—the place where "tactics" are most concentrated—rarely has significant or sustained payoff without a substantial cost.

THE FIVE RINGS MODEL: HOW TO USE IT

When you look at your organization or market through the Five Rings lens, you will find it surprisingly easy to put specific names of individuals, groups, and physical things into each of the Five Rings categories. As you do this, you are "mapping" the system, which means that you are identifying *potential* Centers of Gravity—the targets you may need to affect to achieve your Future Picture.

Figures 9.2 and 9.3 present two typical Five Rings system maps to illustrate the system-mapping concept. The first is a typical *organizational* system; the second, a typical *market* system.

FIVE RINGS MAP OF A TYPICAL ORGANIZATIONAL SYSTEM

Leadership	Key Processes	Infrastructure
Owners/Partners	Communications	Organization Structure
Chairman	Quality	Protocols and Stan-
dards		
	Ideation	
Board of Directors		Installed Bases
	Commercializa-	
CEO	tion	Physical Facilities
COO	Production	Transport Net
CFO	Financing	
Vice Presidents	Staffing	
Executive Committees/	Purchasing	
Councils		
	Distribution	
Informal Leadership		
	Selling	
Peripheral Leaders		
Key Stockholders		
Major JV Partners		
Union Leaders		
Driving Customers		
Driving Suppliers		

Figure 9.2 Five Rings Map of a Typical Organizational System

FIVE RINGS MAP OF A TYPICAL ORGANIZATIONAL SYSTEM

Population	Agents
Customers	Outlets
Management	Divisions
Professionals	Vendors
Technical	Maintenance and Security
Clerical	
Manual	Semiautonomous Groups
Salaried	Purchasing Groups
Hourly	Outsourcers
Language/ethnic	Regulators
Gender	Evangelists
Consultants	

FIVE RINGS MAP OF A TYPICAL MARKET SYSTEM

Leadership	Key Processes	Infrastructure
Market Leaders	Communications	Value Networks
Lead Customers	Ideation	Organization
Lead Associations	Commercialization	Physical Facilities
Peripheral Leaders	Production	Installed Bases
Political Leaders	Purchasing	Transport Net
Finance Leaders	Distribution	
Media Leaders	Selling	
Lead Brands/Ideas	Financing	
	Staffing	
	Energy Conversion	

Figure 9.3 Five Rings Map of a Typical Market System

You can use the generic names we have provided in these tables as thought-starters, but the idea is to replace them with the specific names of individuals, groups, and physical things that exist in your target systems.

Remember that the Five Rings model is simply a planning tool. It allows you to quickly identify Centers of Gravity. If you're not sure about the category in which a Center of Gravity belongs, don't be concerned. Make a choice and move on. What's important is that you get a comprehensive view of the Centers of Gravity in the system.

THE SYSTEM-MAPPING PROCESS

Always begin the mapping process with the largest systems you can reasonably manage, and then work down to smaller subsystems as necessary. In the business world, for example, the largest systems could include the marketplace and the organization itself.

FIVE RINGS MAP OF A TYPICAL MARKET SYSTEM

Population	Agents
Customers	Nonlead Customers
Consumers	Nonlead Competitors
Decision-makers	Supplier Companies
Professionals	Market Suppliers
Owners	Sales Outlets
Employees	Field Purchasing
Innovators	Government Agencies
	Persuaders
	Evangelists
	Actor X

Figure 9.4 shows a series of Five Rings systems that are *fractal*. As you go from a very large system down into its smaller and smaller components, the Five Rings pattern repeats itself each time. The same set of system attributes repeats as you move from the large market, into a particular company, into its board of directors, into its senior executive group, into its divisions, and so on.

The fractal nature of systems means that you can easily analyze any component or subcomponent of a system using the same Five Rings model.

With the relevant systems mapped and with your Centers of Gravity identified, you're now ready to consider the Desired Effects.

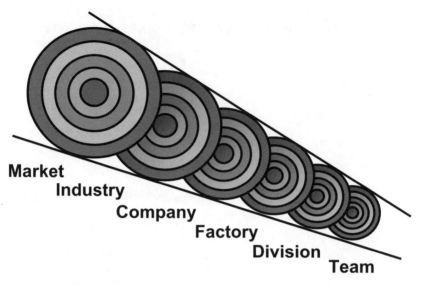

Figure 9.4 Fractal Centers of Gravity

Chapter Debrief: **The Five Rings**

Selecting the right strategic targets is critical to winning in *FastTime*. If you don't get the strategic targets right, it will be difficult, if not impossible, to change the system.

The leaders' role in system targeting is to ensure that everyone focuses on identifying the Centers of Gravity as the first order of business after designing the future.

The Five Rings model presents in visual form the five categories of components common to all dynamic systems: Leadership, Processes, Infrastructure, Population, and Agents.

Each of the rings will contain one or more Centers of Gravity— those components within a system that will have the greatest impact on the entire system if they are altered in any way.

The Five Rings model makes systems thinking usable in the real world.

Map the system by putting specific names of individuals, groups, and physical things into each of the Five Rings categories.

Always begin the mapping process with the largest systems you can reasonably manage, and then work down to smaller subsystems as necessary.

10

Desired Effects

"Target for Effect!"

When John was developing his Five Rings system in Washington in the two years preceding the Gulf War, he emphasized the importance of properly measuring the effect of an attack on the enemy system. When you attack an enemy installation, he taught, the measure of success is not whether it's destroyed, but whether it continues functioning. Only if you succeed in achieving your Desired Effect have you succeeded in the attack.

Many people fail to grasp the extraordinary power of effects-based planning. At the time of the Gulf War, for example, there were many in Washington who still subscribed to the attitude of the intelligence officer described earlier who held that the attacks on electrical facilities had failed because only 10 percent of them had been hit. This reflects the old military view, "The job isn't done until there is nothing but rubble." Needless to say, this was not a systems perspective—and it resulted in a significant waste of resources.

For business, the implications of "effects-based planning" are profound. Suppose you have identified ten Centers of Gravity that you need to change. Are you better off concentrating your available resources on a few of them, or will you be more successful if you spread your resources across a wider range of targets?

Effects-based planning answers that question by helping you ask another: **Which action will result in the greatest probability of having a systemic effect?** In answering that question, a few key principles from earlier chapters apply:

- The extent and probability of system change is directly proportional to both the **number** of Centers of Gravity affected and the **speed** at which they're affected. If you do a "bang-up" job on just a few Centers of Gravity, the system will probably absorb the impact and adapt. That can even happen when you hit your target at the heart of the key "Leadership" ring.

- If you go after **multiple Centers of Gravity,** you have multiple opportunities to create the desired system effects. Each additional Center of Gravity impacted helps to create an exponential increase in total impact across the whole system—a tidal wave of systemic impact.

- A **parallel approach**—attacking many Centers of Gravity at the same time—means some of your actions can fail without affecting your system-changing success. That's because a large percentage of your other actions, occurring simultaneously, may succeed. In short, perfect planning and perfect execution aren't nearly as important in a parallel approach as they would be in a serial approach.

It's not necessary to predict precisely the results of individual attacks. All you need to predict is that the *overall impact* of your parallel efforts will be sufficient to shock the system and will begin to drive it in the desired direction.

LEVERAGING AVAILABLE RESOURCES

Brigadier General (then Lieutenant Colonel) Dave Deptula, one of the brilliant officers on John's staff in the two years before the war, was intimately familiar with "effects-based" targeting and was one of its major proponents. When John began the war-planning process, he called on Dave to join the effort. Dave was to play one of the most important roles in the war, not only as an integral part of the original Checkmate planning team in Washington, but also as the heart of the planning and execution effort in Riyadh.

One of the problems that confronted the planners was how to get the maximum impact from a handful of precision-capable aircraft and missiles in the first hour of the war. The problem especially manifested itself with the Iraqi air defense system. Intelligence revealed that the Iraqis had four major very high-tech operations centers—each backed up by two or more subordinate centers designed to take over the parent center's duties if the parent went out of business.

Most of the Intelligence community was still in the "rubble" mentality. When intelligence analysts were asked how many bombs needed to be dropped on each air defense center, they answered that it would take fifteen to twenty to fully destroy each one. This was an impossible solution. There simply weren't enough available resources—in this instance, Stealth aircraft with precision weapons—to destroy all of these targets in the desired time frame.

Because he understood effects-based planning, Dave came up with the solution. He focused only on achieving the Desired Effect for the air defense centers: Ensure that they were not controlling Iraqi air defense efforts. The Measure of Merit was equally simple— each center must be unable to carry out its functions.

Dave recounts his thinking:

> What to do? The idea struck me that if someone dropped a 2,000-pound bomb on the other end of our building, it might not destroy our facility. But we sure as heck wouldn't be hanging around to finish our coffee.
>
> There was the answer. We didn't need to physically destroy every target; we only needed to render them ineffective—unable to conduct normal operations. Therefore, the emphasis need not be on levels of physical destruction—the

usual measure of success—but rather it should be on creating "system effects."

Dave then used this effects-based planning approach to leverage the available resources. Rather than eight F-117 Stealth fighters acting in unison to destroy each target, a single aircraft could attack each one to render it ineffective. This in turn freed up these scarce resources to use against other critical targets, in particular the biological and chemical weapons sites.

On the opening night of the air campaign, there were forty-two Stealth sorties against eighty targets. With no additional resources, Dave Deptula put forty times as many Iraqi facilities out of operation as would have been possible if the old "rubble" measure of merit had prevailed.

SYSTEM "ENERGY EVENTS"

How do businesses use the concept of effects-based planning? Think about your actions as system "energy events."

When you destroy, disable, or disrupt a Center of Gravity, you create a *negative-energy event*—energy is removed from the Center of Gravity. In Desert Storm, the massive air attacks to disable and disrupt multiple Centers of Gravity like communications and electricity were clearly negative-energy events: The Iraqi system lost energy for its operations.

When you create, improve, or expand a Center of Gravity, you create a *positive-energy event*—energy is added to the Center of Gravity. In the Gulf, the United States led a massive diplomatic campaign aimed at friendly Centers of Gravity like the leaders of Saudi Arabia and other Arab states, as well as coalition allies. These diplomatic efforts were positive-energy events: Energy was being added to allied cooperation and commitment.

Which kind of energy events are appropriate for your Centers of Gravity? In business, almost all attacks should be designed to put energy *into* the Centers of Gravity in your market and organization.

Incidentally, your competitors aren't really your primary targets. That's because your number-one objective is to realize your own Future Picture. You should care little whether your competitors make money or not—as long as you are achieving your Future Picture.

DETERMINING DESIRED EFFECTS

When you understand the concept of effects-based targeting and system energy events, you're ready to develop an action plan for each Center of Gravity.

What effects do you want to impose on the Centers of Gravity you identified when you mapped your system and its Five Rings? How will you measure those effects? What are the associated time frames, actions, and resources?

As you begin the process of determining your Desired Effects, paramount in your mind should be the strategic linkage between two elements: what you do to the Centers of Gravity, and realizing your Future Picture. If you cannot make that connection, you're in danger of squandering valuable resources in activities that are unlikely to produce long-term success.

How do you ensure strategic linkage? *Always* begin by reviewing the Future Picture you have painted—your Key Descriptor statements and the related Measures of Merit. Ask yourself: "For this Future Picture to become reality, how will the Centers of Gravity need to change?"

Once you have identified the key Centers of Gravity for what you are trying to accomplish, you can create an action plan. There are six steps in creating this plan—and the sequence is important:

1. ***Define the Desired Effect***—the specific outcome you want, for each of the Centers of Gravity you have identified. Always think about the strategic linkages—how the Desired Effect will move the Center of Gravity toward your Future Picture. Avoid worrying about the details of the "how-to" at this point—that

will just limit your thinking. Instead, imagine that anything is possible. What would the *ideal* outcome be?

2. *Clarify the Measure of Merit*—how you will know you have achieved the Desired Effect. You tend to get what you measure, so answer this question very carefully: What would *objectively* demonstrate that you've achieved your Desired Effect? When you can succinctly state the answer, you have your Measure of Merit.

3. *Decide on the time frame*—when the Center of Gravity must be affected: now, soon, later, next year. Think in terms of the Future Picture you want to create. For example, a change to the pension plan is probably something that can be done downstream ,whereas getting a strategic customer may be a short-term necessity.

4. *Gather meaningful, reliable information* ("intelligence") about the Center of Gravity—but only as it relates to your Future Picture and creating the Desired Effect. Avoid, at all costs, "vacuuming" information in the hope that some of it may be interesting; this common practice is simply not worth the time and expense.

5. *Develop high-level directions* for achieving the Desired Effect, but do not dictate the tactics. Tactics are the responsibility of campaign planners or others in the organization. For example, in the Gulf War, the high-level directions for a Center of Gravity might have been simply to render it ineffective with little or no risk of collateral damage. The people in the field decided which airplanes, missiles, or bombs were appropriate and how to use them.

6. *Estimate the resource requirements*—skills, mind-sets, authorities, equipment, and funding that you believe are necessary to achieve the Desired Effect. If you know the name of the person or group that should undertake the action, be specific.

A SAMPLE CENTER OF GRAVITY ACTION PLAN

Here's a sample Center of Gravity action plan for our hypothetical firm, FastWin Corporation.

The situation: One of the Key Descriptors in FastWin's Future Picture is to be a market driver and leader. FastWin's CEO recognizes that his cadre of senior executives do not understand the trends in the market, nor are they acting rapidly and aggressively enough to make FastWin a market leader.

Center of Gravity: FastWin's senior executive group (a Center of Gravity in the Leadership ring).

Desired Effect: A critical mass of FastWin's senior executives understands emerging market opportunities and moves rapidly and aggressively to seize those opportunities.

Measure of Merit: FastWin's strategic position in the market improves substantially within two years, measured by a predetermined increase in profitability and growth of its operations.

Time frame: Immediate start with first visible results in six months.

Actions: Develop and deliver a fast-paced, information-rich, action-learning program that educates senior executives about the market, and builds the desired mind-set and skill set necessary to be both market drivers and market leaders.

Resources: Time (for the CEO and executive team to oversee development of the program); funds (for designing and delivering the program); and expert personnel (selection of experts in executive-action learning design).

Remember that the overall goal is to affect the whole system, and that this particular Center of Gravity—FastWin's senior executive group—is only one of the Centers of Gravity that will need to be affected to ensure success.

THE POWER OF PRECISION TARGETING: THE "TRIM-TAB" EFFECT

The fractal nature of systems means that you can easily analyze *any* Center of Gravity using the Five Rings model. But why should you take the time to go into this level of detail? Here's why:

The more precisely defined the target, the less energy is required to affect it. A good analogy can be found in the way a large ship is controlled. A ship is a mechanical system and its rudder is a major Center of Gravity. If you want to change the ship's direction, you could move its rudder. But the mass of the ship is enormous, and the momentum so great that the ship may take a mile or more to turn or stop. Especially at high speed, a tremendous amount of energy is required to move the rudder. But imagine a ship that has, on the back edge of the rudder, another tiny rudder, a trim-tab. A much smaller amount of force is required to move the trim-tab (the rudder's Center of Gravity), which in turn moves the rudder (the system's Center of Gravity) in the desired direction and changes the direction of the ship (the system).

In the Desert Storm air campaign, the Checkmate team first identified Iraq's key Centers of Gravity, one of which, as previously mentioned, was its electrical system. A quick Five Rings analysis of that system revealed all the typical components: *Leadership Ring*—the managers who controlled it; *Processes Ring*—heat- and steam-producing facilities, electrical generators, and transformers; *Infrastructure Ring*—power lines; *Population Ring*—a variety of different kinds of people ranging from engineers to manual laborers; *Agents Ring*—repair and security teams.

What observations could be made very quickly about each of these?

Leadership Ring: Managers: If you could convince them all to shut down their grid areas, the job is done. Of course, finding and convincing them might take a long time. Not likely.

Processes Ring: Heat- and steam-producing facilities: These are robust structures that are hard to knock out, and, in addition, the Iraqis might quickly find work-arounds to get them back into operation.

Processes Ring: Generators: The obvious choice, but the obvious choice was wrong because replacing the generators after the war would be a lengthy and expensive process that did not comport with the Future Picture.

Processes Ring: Transformers: Eureka! Would be easy to hit, have a devastating impact, be hard to repair in the short term, but easy and relatively cheap to repair after the war. Matches Future Picture.

Infrastructure Ring: Power lines: Thousands of miles of them and quite easy to repair.

Population Ring: The electrical workers: Not much known about them and no easy way to reach them.

Agents Ring: Repair and security teams: Elusive, easily shifted from one location to another, and very hard to hit.

Note that it was not necessary to gather voluminous data to go through this analysis, and note how quickly it led to the right answer— hit the transformers *in the Processes ring.*

Because the Checkmate team used the Open Planning approach, there was someone in the room who had enough knowledge about Iraq's national electrical systems to go through the Five Rings analysis described above. After this basic analysis was complete, the information gathering began. Intelligence analysts were given the task of telling the team exactly where the transformers were located. Note that the analysts now had a very finite task instead of the infinite one that results when someone says, "Tell me everything about electrical systems."

PRIORITIZING CENTERS OF GRAVITY

The first phase of any strategic operation, which could be a day, a week, or a month, should shock the system—the *whole* system. Remember that to overwhelm system resistance, you'll need to affect many Centers of Gravity, preferably one or more in each ring. That means orchestrating your available resources—people, capital, equipment, and so on—to simultaneously affect as many system leverage points as possible.

Of course, it's very rare for an organization to have sufficient resources to attack every Center of Gravity at the same time. With constrained resources, what do you do? Here's what not to do: Do *not* give up because you can't hit everything at the same time, and do *not* plan a series of one-by-one (serial) attacks.

Leadership	Processes	Infrastructure	Population	Agents
▷ 10	▷ 10	▷ 10	▷ 10	▷ 10
▷ 9	▷ 9	▷ 9	▷ 9	▷ 9
▷ 8	▷ 8	▷ 8	▷ 8	▷ 8
▷ 7	▷ 7	▷ 7	▷ 7	▷ 7
▷ 6	▷ 6	▷ 6	▷ 6	▷ 6
▷ 5	▷ 5	▷ 5	▷ 5	▷ 5
▷ 4	▷ 4	▷ 4	▷ 4	▷ 4
▷ 3	▷ 3	▷ 3	▷ 3	▷ 3
▷ 2	▷ 2	▷ 2	▷ 2	▷ 2
▷ 1	▷ 1	▷ 1	▷ 1	▷ 1

Figure 10.1 Master Attack Plan

Figure 10.1 shows fifty targets that have been mapped using the Five Rings process—and laid out in vertical table form for simplicity. For now, think of these five vertical columns as capturing an entire system with the Centers of Gravity in the vertical columns.

Suppose that you want to attack this system and change it rapidly to meet your objectives, but have only ten "bombs" available. The solution is to select a cross section of Centers of Gravity as illustrated Figure 10.1. You will attack these targets and attack them in parallel with as much simultaneity as possible. If you hit most of them, you will begin the process of shocking the system.

Before the system has recovered, attack the cross section of targets between the first and second line to intensify the shock and accelerate the system toward paralysis. You could have additional phases as required.

The bottom line is this: The key to "moving the system" is to *prioritize the Centers of Gravity* and address them in phases. Plan for integrated, "pulsed attacks" that will move the whole system in the desired direction. How you carry those out is the subject of our next chapter—parallel campaigns.

Chapter Debrief: Desired Effects

Once you have mapped the system, determine the Desired Effects to impose on the Centers of Gravity you have identified.

A system "energy event" is what occurs when you attack a Center of Gravity. After your action, energy is either added or taken away from the Center of Gravity.

Ensure that there is strategic linkage—a direct connection between the Desired Effects and realizing your Future Picture.

Create an action plan for each Center of Gravity. There are six steps in creating this plan:

Define the Desired Effect.
Clarify the Measure of Merit.
Decide on the time frame.
Gather meaningful, reliable information .
Develop high-level directions.
Estimate the resource requirements.

You can analyze a Center of Gravity fractally (level by level) using the Five Rings model. The more precisely defined the target, the less amount of energy is required to affect it.

To optimize resources, prioritize the Centers of Gravity and address them in phases. Plan for integrated, "pulsed attacks" that will move the whole system in the desired direction.

The first phase of any strategic operation, which could be a day, a week, or a month, should shock the system—the whole system.

PROMETHEUS PROCESS

IMPERATIVE THREE

CAMPAIGN TO WIN

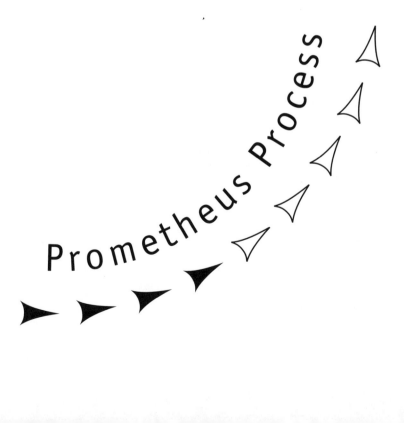

11

Parallel Campaigns

> "The parallel approach accelerates results and increases the probability of success."

Once you've defined your Desired Effects, the next step is to apply your resources as effectively as possible to achieve them. You accomplish this through a robust, adaptable organizational form we call "parallel campaigns."

A campaign is a temporary assemblage of resources (people, money, and equipment) concentrated against the targeted Centers of Gravity. Campaigns have a laserlike focus on getting results as rapidly as possible and changing system energy levels.

When multiple campaigns operate in parallel with the same strategic intent, the sheer velocity of concentrated actions increases the odds of success. The measure of a campaign's success is not the quantity, or even the quality, of its efforts. The measure is the speed and depth of results.

The parallel campaign approach is the key to rapidly and deeply changing results throughout the system. It has two essential elements: multiplicity—many Centers of Gravity are affected; and simultaneity—the effects occur at about the same time.

Parallel campaigns allow you to concentrate for success. You put all of your resources—people, money, and equipment—on the table and then intelligently focus them against the right priorities. The parallel campaign approach usually requires fewer resources than a serial approach because multiple actions shorten the duration of effort—and as the saying goes, time is money.

Parallel campaigns are not only fast, they have the flexibility to "turn on a dime" when circumstances warrant. This capacity for adapting in real time is crucial. If you're not in real time, you won't survive in a hyper-speed world.

Parallel campaigns are an antidote to bureaucracy because they're not designed to be permanent. Quite the reverse. Termination points are established in advance. A campaign continues only until the desired system effects have been realized. Then it disbands, and the resources it employed are available to be applied elsewhere.

In a parallel campaign, turf battles recede since there's less time for them. And as interdisciplinary, cross-functional groups orchestrate their resources, they tend to create a culture of collaboration.

PARALLEL CAMPAIGNS @ MOTOROLA

In Desert Storm, high-velocity parallel campaigns were used to rapidly disable a country. At Motorola, this same approach was used to rapidly *enable* a whole new organization.

For years, Motorola had been organized into separate product lines: a paging unit, a two-way radio unit, a cell-phone unit, a cellular infrastructure unit, and a satellite unit. The problem with this structure was that the market, driven by demand for mobile communications, was changing very rapidly and Motorola was having difficulty meeting the changing needs of its major customers. These customers were consolidating and, at the same time, were looking for more integrated communication solutions.

Meanwhile, demand was exploding, competition was intensifying, and end-user expectations were increasing. People wanted cheaper, smaller, and more universal devices. They no longer wanted to carry around multiple personal-productivity devices—a pager, a cell phone, a palm top computer—to meet their mobility needs. They wanted these devices and the related services to be integrated.

But Motorola had an organizational problem. Because the product lines were effectively operational silos, it was difficult if not impossible to offer customers an integrated solution. So the decision was made to create a fully integrated business unit—the Communications Enterprise—that would bring everything together.

Sandy Ogg, Corporate Vice President and Director of the company's Office of Leadership, was part of the founding leadership team of the new organization.

Deciding to create the Communications Enterprise group was the easy part. Making change happen was a challenge that required a rapid, massive change-management effort. After consulting with us, Ogg decided to apply many of the concepts presented in these pages. Sandy recalls his thought process:

> While Motorola is certainly not as big a system as the country of Iraq, it is, by organizational standards, quite large, with 80,000 employees and $22 billion in sales.
>
> What are some of the big leverage points (Centers of Gravity) in a system like that? We identified leaders, core business processes and structure, and big revenue hitters and cost drivers as priorities.
>
> Our next step was to develop five parallel campaigns with enough energy and focus to overwhelm the leverage points in an integrated way. The key was to have the campaigns tightly focused and not just have a bunch of initiatives. We had a few big ones designed to overwhelm the system.

How does Motorola—or any company—go about organizing such an effort? The answer is to commission campaign teams. The first step is to select an overall Campaign Orchestrator.

THE CAMPAIGN ORCHESTRATOR

In a perfect world with a perfectly developed system map and few resource constraints, campaign teams could execute their campaign plans without reference to other teams. In the real world, of course, there are overlaps among the campaigns, resources are limited, and the actions of one campaign can affect other campaigns positively or negatively.

To achieve maximum system impact, campaigns need to be *strategically integrated.* Someone must be responsible for dealing with these issues. That's the job of the Campaign Orchestrator: to ensure that each campaign moves rapidly in parallel with the others and that, collectively, they achieve the desired strategic results. In short, the Campaign Orchestrator assumes overall responsibility for the success of the campaigns. The role is not directive in the sense of telling people how to do their jobs, but it does ensure that everyone is meeting timelines, that people are getting approvals they need in real time, and that efforts are coordinated.

Good Orchestrators share some common characteristics. They make rapid, decisive decisions; they do what it takes to liberate people from the bureaucratic constraints that inhibit creativity and momentum; they are able to maintain a strategic perspective in the midst of dynamic change.

To succeed, the Orchestrator needs the authority to make decisions almost instantly on most campaign issues without reference to higher authority; if the Orchestrator is merely serving as a data and information forwarder, there is little value added. To make real-time decisions, the Orchestrator needs to be constantly available to the campaign's teams to answer questions, to provide (or get) answers, and to make strategic choices when necessary.

John Warden played the role of Orchestrator in the planning of the Desert Storm air campaign. As the leader of the Checkmate planning team, he didn't give orders but rather told the team to "get busy and flesh out the plan as rapidly as possible." With little debate, the team self-organized and divided tasks among small groups that could react quickly to changing events. John saw himself as a conductor of planning process. "I didn't own the concert hall or tell the musicians how to play. My role was to lead the information symphony."

THE CAMPAIGN ROOM

The Orchestrator's job is easiest (and the parallel campaigns most likely to succeed quickly) when there is a central campaign room that is the focus of most campaign activity. This facility is invaluable in keeping everyone involved with the campaigns, and others in the organization, up to speed on what is happening and allows them to see how they may be able to contribute.

When John first pulled together a large number of people to begin the Gulf War planning process that was to produce the plan approved by General Schwarzkopf forty-eight hours later, he chose one of his division's large briefing rooms in the basement of the Pentagon. What became known as the "Campaign Room" was not pretty or elegant, but it accommodated a lot of standing people and it had plenty of wall space. The wall space in this case was especially good because it consisted of multiple sliding panels with white boards, corkboards, and maps that could be slid back and forth as circumstances demanded. This allowed the information to be displayed in such a way that everyone could see it at the same time, and always see it in a total context.

Most people try to do serious planning in small conference rooms that have little usable wall space and that must be vacated at the end of the day. They start with terrible physical handicaps: too small a room; too little wall space to allow contextual display of information; and an obvious transitoriness that diminishes the importance of the effort and greatly complicates the work if it doesn't get done in a single day. So important is the campaign room concept that we usually insist that our clients agree to create a campaign room as a condition of our working with them.

What if you don't have space available for the campaign room? If you consider it a priority, you will probably find a solution. For example, one of our clients, a major supplier to McDonald's, leased a double-wide mobile office trailer and parked it behind one of its plants. It provided the necessary space, but there was an added benefit. From the moment that mobile office arrived, everyone knew that something serious and very different was going on.

Where is the Orchestrator's office? John Warden put his desk in the middle of the campaign room, which remained the heart of the planning effort through the end of the war. The room was noisy and sometimes chaotic, but by being right there in the middle, John was instantly available to anyone of any rank who needed a decision or an answer or who had a question. Having someone right there on the spot made a huge difference in the velocity of the plan development.

Contrast this to the typical approach, in which the person in charge of planning sends groups off to work for hours (or days, or weeks, or months) with only general instructions; when they return, the response too frequently is, "Good work, but why did you not . . . ?" If you want rapid results, remove the impediments to real-time communications and decision-making.

VIRTUAL CAMPAIGN ROOMS

What do you do when campaign members are not colocated? It is more challenging for the Orchestrator if the campaign members are physically dispersed, but it is still possible to have a virtual campaign room where issues are discussed and where problems and solutions are posted for all to see.

For example, one of our clients created an online database that allowed everyone to access whatever level of detail they needed about the activities in every change campaign. No one had to call a staff meeting to get updated, nor was it necessary for people to waste valuable time preparing reports. At any time, anybody in the company, working in any of its facilities, had access to the same campaign status information. They could see and comment on all the plans, and stay abreast of all the bottlenecks and breakthroughs.

THE CAMPAIGN MIND-SET

Parallel campaigns are very powerful, even if done only reasonably well, and they pay faster and higher dividends than traditional organizational approaches. However, successful campaigning requires a new mind-set.

The Orchestrator and the leaders of campaigns "own" the targeted Centers of Gravity. This means that they are responsible for achieving the Desired Effect in the planned time frame. If they do not have the resources, then they find them. Their success is measured not by the quantity or even the quality of their efforts, but by their results.

In high-velocity campaigns, rank and position have little meaning. The focus is on the quality of ideas and the capacity to make things happen quickly. The campaign organizational structure is very flat and creates a span of control far larger than most would think possible or desirable.

We have found that good campaign Orchestrators can easily "manage" (but not micromanage) even hundreds of people. One of the secrets to their success is using two unique approaches to communication: the Three-Echelon Rule and the Red Team.

THREE-ECHELON RULE

People in general do a very poor job of communicating instructions to people who work for or with them. Think of how many times you have been in a long staff meeting where the majority were not taking notes. You listened to intense conversations, and decisions made were either murky, conditional, or based on nuance. When those attending the long planning meeting returned to tell their subordinates what had taken place, they provided a two-minute summary, which was probably not quite correct. Shortly thereafter, one of the subordinates—who does not understand why something is to be done—asks the person who attended the meeting. That person also does not really know, but is unwilling to get back to the people who were at the meeting, for fear of looking silly. Conse-quently, the subordinate goes off and does the best job possible. It may be a really great job from that person's perspective, but it may bear scant relationship to what those at the original staff meeting had envisaged.

Well over a century ago, the Prussian military solved this prob-lem by developing and putting into effect what we call the Three-Echelon Rule. The Three-Echelon Rule tells you to have at least three organizational echelons present anytime you are doing any serious planning or are about to make any decisions. If people are present at a meeting, they pick up the nuances and the implica-tions far better than anyone can report them orally or in writing. Later, when these lower-echelon people find themselves confronted with a situation not anticipated at the planning meeting, they understand enough of the intent and the thinking to make a smart decision that is in consonance with the desired goals.

Some groups are reluctant to use the Three-Echelon Rule because "it takes too much time to get everyone together." These, of course, are the very people who cannot understand why their subordinates never seem to do things right, or why no one will make a decision. In actuality, the Three-Echelon approach is far faster and cheaper than the other approaches—especially when you measure against results. For a fast-moving, dynamic organization, Three-Echelon communication is a necessity.

THE RED TEAM

Early in the high-speed Gulf War planning process, John became concerned that his group would fall into a "groupthink" mode in which it would accept a course of action merely because no one wanted to stand in the way of progress.

In addition to the concern over groupthink, John also wanted to make sure that nothing consequential was being overlooked. After all, the Checkmate group was planning something that would have life-and-death consequences for thousands of people.

To avoid groupthink and inadvertent error, John created a "Red Team," a group of people who were institutionally charged with telling their colleagues everything they were doing wrong. (When people are institutionally charged to criticize, they do a far better job of it than when they are part of a planning team.)

While remaining fully conversant with everything the Checkmate team was planning, the Red Team put itself in the place of the world's smartest opponent and told the planning team how the world's smartest opponent would keep the proposed plan from working.

"Being on the receiving end of a Red Team can be a disconcerting experience," John recalls. "The first few times the Red Team challenges what you and your smart associates have spent hours or days putting together, your tendency is to bristle and reject. This, of course, is not the right response. The right response is to evaluate the Red Team's conclusions objectively and to re-examine your plan without hesitation. In addition, whenever the Red Team comes up with something that the world's smartest opponent could do, the right response is to change your plan in order to preempt the opponent's ability to do it."

Some organizations may not have the personnel available to create a dedicated Red Team. An alternative in this case is to tell everyone on the planning team—at the completion of the plan or at the end of a phase of planning—to put on their figurative Red Team hats and challenge everything to which they have just agreed. The results are impressive; normally, as much as a quarter of the agreement is back on the table. After a short while, about half of this will be resolved in a new way, while everyone finally understands and genuinely agrees with the other half.

Either approach is fine. What is not good is having no Red Team.

CAMPAIGNS IN REVIEW

In the simplest sense, campaigns are about getting the job done. In the Prometheus Process, this means bringing a lot of pressure on the system very, very rapidly to break its elastic limit and move it into a new state. This will require that there be multiple efforts—multiple campaigns under way, each doing something different.

Campaigns must, however, remain strategically aligned and focused on sets of Centers of Gravity. To succeed, they must be high-velocity operations. Understand that velocity and speed are not the same thing. Speed has no direction associated with it; velocity is not only how fast you are traveling but also *to where* you are traveling. Many organizations are speedy; few are high-velocity.

Remember, as campaign velocity increases, the probability of success and the productivity of available resources grow proportionately. The campaign process we have talked about so far is one that can stand alone. For optimal results, and to have the highest probability of success across the board, you will need to *Organize for Success*—which is the subject of the next chapter.

Chapter Debrief: Parallel Campaigns

A campaign is a temporary assemblage of resources (people, money, and equipment) that has a laserlike focus on getting results as rapidly as possible.

The parallel campaign approach has two essential elements: *multiplicity*—many Centers of Gravity are affected; and *simultaneity*—the effects occur at about the same time.

The measure of a campaign's success is the speed and depth of results.

The Campaign Orchestrator ensures that the campaigns move rapidly in parallel and achieve the desired strategic results.

To succeed, the Campaign Orchestrator needs the authority to make decisions almost instantly on most campaign issues without reference to higher authority.

Good Orchestrators make rapid, decisive decisions, liberate people from bureaucratic constraints, and maintain a strategic perspective in the midst of dynamic change.

It's important to have a central campaign room that is the focus of most campaign activity. This room can be physical or virtual.

Rank and position have little meaning in a campaign environment. The organizational structure is flat and the focus is on the quality of ideas and the capacity to make things happen quickly. One of the secrets to successful campaigning is to use the Three-Echelon Rule and the Red Team:

- Three-Echelon Rule: Anytime you are doing any serious planning or decision-making, have at least three organizational echelons present.
- Red Team: This is a group of people whose job is to challenge assumptions and flag potential problems in advance.

12

Organizing for Success

> "The structures of the past rarely fit the exigencies of the future."

In the early days of the Roman Empire, its leaders organized for success by basing most of the Imperial Legions in Rome, and keeping them ready for dispatch to wherever they were needed for seizing an opportunity or solving a problem. Traveling a superbly designed Roman road system, the well-trained, fully equipped legions could reach the periphery of the empire with remarkable speed. As soon as the situation was handled, the legions returned to Rome, ready again to respond rapidly in any direction.

Executing your campaign plans is a similar challenge. Like the Romans, you need a dynamic structure that allows you to be fast, nimble, and continuously self-adapting. You need a structure that makes it easier to assemble the right resources and to deploy them at the right times against the right Centers of Gravity.

The concept of the campaign discussed in the last chapter also provides a highly valuable approach to a robust, adaptable organizational form that becomes the basic building block of the *FastTime* organization—a temporary collection of resources (people, money, and equipment) focused on achieving a specific strategic result.

But for campaigns to operate successfully, some structural change in the organization may be necessary.

NEW SITUATION, NEW STRUCTURE

How do you ensure that your campaigns realize their full potential? Create an organizational structure that will support, rather than hinder, their success.

Organizational structure is important because it shapes individual behaviors and causes certain patterns of events to reoccur. By changing the structure, you can create new behaviors and new patterns of events that will increase the probability of success.

Organizational structure is a choice, not a given. There's no law that says, "When faced with new challenges or new opportunities, you must rely on the current organizational structure to address them." That kind of rigidity would be ridiculous. Yet that's often the unspoken assumption. Most organizations find it difficult to make fast, fundamental structural changes. But is maintaining the status quo a sustainable alternative?

When you design a new strategy, develop a new kind of product, or face new forms of competition, your old organizational structure is obsolete for a very simple reason: It was designed for a situation that no longer exists. So there's an urgent need for a new structure, one that will increase your probability of success in the new situation.

Clayton Christensen, in *The Innovator's Dilemma,* offers a good case study of the value of "organizing for success." In the late 1980s and early 1990s, Hewlett-Packard (HP) had a highly profitable laser-printer business, but was also interested in pursuing inkjet technology. The traditional bureaucratic approach would have been to make inkjets a part of the existing printer division. However, someone anticipated that the managers of the existing printer division, which was essentially a laser-printer operation, would not optimize the inkjet's potential. Why? The laser people would tend to measure the inkjet by laser standards and find it wanting. It was a very different kind of product with different measures of success: a low-margin, low-resolution product targeted primarily at the consumer market.

The company decided to establish a completely separate inkjet group in another city hundreds of miles away. There, the new group was free to develop its own products, choose its own measures of success, and approach the market in a fiercely competitive way. If the inkjet business cannibalized the laser business, so be it. HP as a whole would win in any event. As it turned out, the news was good for all concerned. The HP inkjet became wildly successful while HP lasers continued to prosper.

STRATEGIC FLEXIBILITY

Because the world is changing so fast, your plans—and your organization—must be even more dynamic. A term for this is "strategic flexibility"—the ability, when necessary, to quickly change direction.

Consider what occurred with Microsoft in the mid-1990s. Thanks to the success of Windows, the company was growing exponentially. When the World Wide Web first appeared, Bill Gates considered it to be little more than a curiosity: "If you'd asked me then if most TV ads will have URLs [Web addresses] in them, I would have laughed."

Then, suddenly, the Web exploded. "Some 20 million people were surfing the Net without using Microsoft software," reported *Business Week*. But that was not Microsoft's biggest concern. Sun Microsystems had developed a Web-based programming language—Java—that directly challenged Windows' hegemony in the PC market.

Fortunately for Microsoft employees and shareholders, Gates was well aware of how market-leading companies tend to stumble when the dynamics of the market fundamentally shift. That stumble had happened to IBM, General Motors, and many others, but Gates was determined it would not happen to Microsoft.

In just six months, Microsoft changed direction and reinvented itself from the ground up. All of its PC software was "Web-ized." New, Web-focused products, from browsers to servers, were developed by the Internet Platform & Tools Division—which employed more programmers than Netscape, Yahoo!, and the next five Net upstarts combined. "What they're doing is decisive, quick, breathtaking," said Jeffrey Katzenberg of DreamWorks SKG. (Some of Microsoft's actions were to have a downside, giving the Justice Department ammunition for its antitrust suit just a few years later. Had Microsoft used the Prometheus systems approach, the company could have foreseen the threat and been in a position to preempt it.)

You may be thinking, "Strategic flexibility sounds great in theory, but our people won't support something like that." Ask yourself this: Is maintaining the status quo really a viable alternative to strategic change?

NEW TECHNOLOGIES, NEW STRUCTURES

Whenever you are confronted with a new objective, new situation, or new technology, you have two choices: Make the old organization work or create a new one. Most people opt for the former, and it frequently fails. Conversely, people who create new organizations, even if they are not very good, have a tendency to be successful.

Case in point: In the 1930s, both the Germans and the French were developing new technologies, including new tanks and new airplanes. On balance, the French technology was probably somewhat superior to the German. But the French leaders made a not-so-bold decision to use their new tanks and airplanes within the old organizational structure, which simply spread them out all over France. The Germans, on the other hand, created an entirely new organization designed to take full advantage of the potential power of tanks and airplanes working together.

When the Germans invaded France in May of 1940, their fast,

focused new organization quickly overwhelmed the slow, decen-
tralized French. A large part of Germany's success was due not to
more or better soldiers and equipment, but rather to the superiority
of the German organizational structure.

The underlying rule: The odds favor those who, when faced
with new objectives, new technologies, or new situations, create a
new organization, rather than try to adapt the old structure.

RESISTING CHANGE

The concept of creating a new organizational structure when confronted with technological change is straightforward. More challenging are the cultural shifts required at every level of the organization.

Consider the resistance to the changes that come with new
technology—a seemingly universal malady. A few years ago, Dell
Computer Corporation released a study that revealed the scope of
the problem. Despite America's long-standing lead in technology
innovation, 55 percent of all those polled remained resistant, even
phobic, about taking advantage of technology in their everyday
lives.

Resistance to new technology is also common in the military
world. Horse-cavalry officers fought vigorously against the aban-
donment of horses even into the 1950s, a good fifty years after it
was obvious to everyone else that the day of the horse was done. As
late as 1892, traditionalists in the U.S. Navy were fighting for a
return from steam power to wind power. The pressure was so strong
that it required the ongoing attention of a senior officer close to the
Secretary of the Navy, Captain John Melville (brother of Herman
Melville of *Moby-Dick* fame) to prevent it from happening. It seems
the traditionalists were upset because coal dust made it impossible
to maintain ships in their pristine appearance—a Measure of Merit
that seems bizarre now, but that kind of thinking, under a different
guise, is prevalent today in most businesses.

One of the real powers of new information technologies, and one of the most important reasons for having an organization that can respond with strategic flexibility, is the ability these technologies give a user to orchestrate multiple events over a very wide continuum of time and space. These revolutionary advances in technology also make it possible to do many things more accurately, in a fraction of the time, and with results many times greater than previously achieved. Fast, precise, parallel operations are now eminently viable. And this changes the strategy game—for you and your competitors—in a big way.

Because of the fast rate of change, information is now like a perishable food. Use it or lose it—its shelf life is extremely short. You can't hide information away somewhere and expect it to have value weeks or months later.

The organization that wins will be the one that exploits information faster than its competitors. To exploit information rapidly, you need to embrace the new technologies that allow you to store, process, and disseminate information using state-of-the-art techniques. An organizational infrastructure designed to deliver real-time information is also absolutely essential. This should include a wide range of electronic tools—from e-mail and Web sites to live video and Webcasts—in order to bathe everyone in as much information as possible.

But technology is not the ultimate success factor. The real key is an *intelligent* attitude toward information.

One definition of intelligence is "the ability to understand and deal with new situations." The arrival of the Information Age certainly qualifies as a new situation, and everyone in business must deal with one of the key implications: Real-time information is lifeblood in a hyper-change world.

Hoarding or even slowing down information flow in your organization must be considered a sin. When people are forced to make uninformed decisions, it almost always costs the organization more than it saves. An organization that is behind the real-time information curve is blind.

During the Gulf War, Saddam continued to threaten the "mother of all battles" long after his forces had been crippled. Was it pure braggadocio or plain propaganda? The most likely explanation is that, with his information apparatus destroyed, he was basing his statements on information from before the war began. That information was obsolete as soon as the first missiles hit their targets.

In contrast, U.S. forces not only preserved their information flow, they enhanced it. John Warden's Checkmate group in the Pentagon was linked closely in cyberspace with Dave Deptula's Black Hole group in Riyadh. When Checkmate action officers came across a piece of information about Iraqi activity, they would immediately convey it along with suggested targeting plans to the Black Hole group. Time after time, the target had been destroyed days before the intelligence bureaucracy was able to present the information to Deptula's group in Riyadh.

In 1999, Motorola Corporation embarked on an aggressive plan to build profitability and stockholder equity. Motorola's Corporate Vice President and Director, Sandy Ogg, explains how they shared information:

> We created an internal "CNN" broadcast over our Intranet, going out to all of our people, to report campaign progress to date and explain the next set of objectives and how they could contribute. Like the daily war briefings in Desert Storm, our senior officers would tell our employees what had been "bombed" so far and what the next targets would be.
>
> The total audience was about 80,000, and 15,000 were receiving the streaming video directly through their desktop computers. People in the factories normally gathered into large rooms convenient to their work sites.
>
> Because of the importance of everyone knowing the game plan, we actually bussed people into theaters for the first broadcast. Every broadcast was live. The business leader, who was Merle Gilmore, would have about thirty

minutes of prepared comments and then people would e-mail their questions in and then he would answer the questions in real time.

The concept of Three-Echelon communications also applies here. A prime way to impede information is to insist on serial transmission. Instead of being *broadcast,* ideas that need to be shared in an organization are passed through layer after layer, trickling down slowly and often becoming distorted in the process.

It's like the old party game of "Telephone"—Maria whispers a story to Carl, Carl whispers it to Sue, Sue to Bill, and so on down the line. Everyone repeats what they think they heard, as best they can recall. By the time the story reaches the last person, it's a very different story from the one first told.

In business, the same thing happens. When those who attended a meeting return to report what's just taken place, the information gets passed down the line as depicted in Figure 12.1.

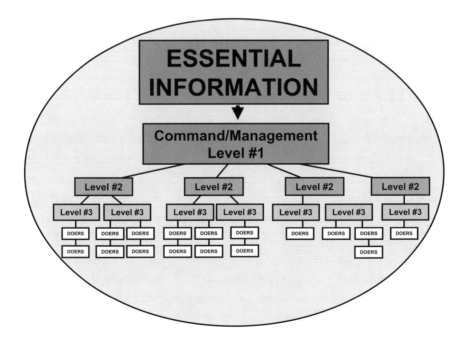

Figure 12.1 The Serial Flow of Essential Information

To expand the process described earlier, the Level 1 people who were present at the meeting pass on only a small part of what was discussed, some of it inaccurately, down to the next echelon, Level 2, which ends up with much less of the essential information. The Level 2 people in turn pass on only a small part of what they have received to Level 3. Finally, Level 3 people pass on what they think they heard to the "Doers"—the people who actually use the information to do their work. Notice the very minute amount of essential information that made its way through the filtering process compared to what was discussed during the Level 1 executive group meeting.

That's the problem with filtering. What can you do about it?

Here are three guidelines to accelerate information flow and support *FastTime* operations:

- Have an open attitude about information—share it; seek it.
- If the hierarchy slows you down, go around it—if necessary, create an alternative communication channel.
- Avoid serial information dissemination—involve as many people, firsthand, as you can.

THE COST OF CHANGE

Structural changes have emotional and financial costs, and should not be lightly undertaken. The best approach to planning and executing major change is to use the Open Planning process. If many people have contributed to creating a new Grand Strategy and if none has been excluded, everyone will be far more willing to help create new organizational structures; these structures, in turn, will allow them to participate in realizing the Future Picture. As pointed out elsewhere, the surest way to create morale and efficiency problems is to plan new organization structures in secret. First, nothing like this remains secret for long; and second, people will begin acting to protect themselves against the threats they think are emerging.

New organizational structures should, of course, be directly linked to the Key Descriptors you painted in your Future Picture. For example, you may have painted a picture of a company that will have entrepreneurial employees and cycle times that are a fraction of what they currently are. If this is what you really want, it is hard to justify sticking with your traditional decision processes that require multiple approvals for the smallest new effort.

HIGH-VELOCITY CHANGE

When you decide that new objectives, or new technologies, justify organizational change, the velocity with which you move becomes very important.

At first glance, the change curve depicted in Figure 12.2 follows the pattern of the Time Value graphs presented earlier. Here again, the probability of success is high if action—parallel action—is taken quickly, but declines as time passes without successfully creating change. Have we not all seen vivid examples of negative things happening as a change operation stretches out over time?

The point is this: Organizational change calls for rapid parallel operations that will shock the system into moving in the right

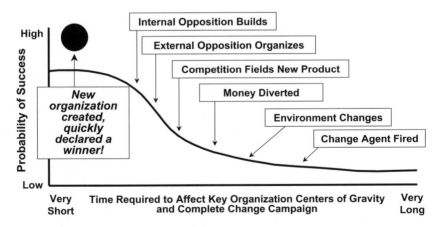

Figure 12.2 High-Velocity Change

direction before it can muster its natural resistance to change. Change experts tell us that 75 percent or more of all major change efforts, including mergers, fail to accomplish their goals.

One of the prime reasons for this high failure rate is the serial nature of most change efforts. Organizational change efforts are subject to the same laws of probability that affect any system-change attempt. This means the more serial you are and the more time you take (the two go together), the lower your probability of success. In addition, the energy expenditure and pain associated with organizational change goes up rapidly over time.

ORGANIZE FOR SUCCESS

Organizing for success is essential; in fact, it's difficult to overemphasize that organizational structures must be designed to solve today's and tomorrow's challenges, not yesterday's. Very simply, the ideal organizational structure is "no structure after its time." In other words, the organizational structure must be formed and re-formed to address emerging opportunities. Whatever the form, it must be very dynamic; a static organizational structure by definition cannot be correct for tomorrow. A dynamic organizational structure allows you to assemble the right resources (people, money, and equipment) to realize a specific objective by affecting the right Centers of Gravity.

Although there are many potentially good structures, a great, dynamic organization like a great orchestra. The leader is available in real time to provide necessary direction (but not to tell the players how to play). A dynamic organization has few or no physical barriers to interaction and knowledge flow. Everyone has a pretty good idea what everyone else is doing and knows how his or her job relates to the Grand Strategy and to other jobs.

When we've organized for success, we are ready to address an area the neglect of which has caused much grief—how to end a project, a product, a business unit, or even an entire company so that maximum returns are realized for everyone involved.

Chapter Debrief: Organizing for Success

To ensure that your campaigns realize their full potential, create an organizational structure that will support, rather than hinder, their success.

Organizational structure is important because it shapes individual behaviors and causes certain patterns of events to reoccur.

When faced with new objectives, new technologies, or new situations, the odds favor those who create a new organization, not those who try to adapt the old structure.

One of the real powers of new information technologies is their ability to manage multiple events over a very wide continuum of time and space.

Because of the rate of change, the shelf life of information is extremely short. The organization that wins will be the one that exploits information faster than its competitors.

Accelerate information flow and support *FastTime* operations by:

- having an open, "share it/seek it" attitude about information;
- creating alternative communications channels when bureaucracy slows you down;
- avoiding serial information dissemination.

PROMETHEUS PROCESS

IMPERATIVE FOUR

FINISH WITH FINESSE

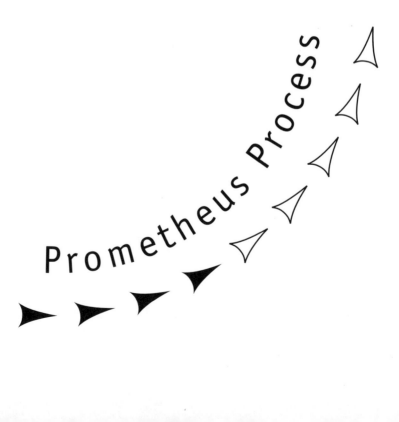

13

The Endgame

"Don't begin until you plan the end."

"All earthly things have a beginning and an end," states the eighth Promethic law, and the ninth law tells us, "Specific ends can be crafted with specific actions just as specific futures can be crafted with specific means." In essence, these two laws tell us that we ought to plan the endgame as carefully as we plan the "start game."

That sounds simple enough, yet very few states, companies, or individuals spend any serious effort on the endgame despite thousands of years of history teaching us this lesson.

You might think that efforts devoted to endgame planning are of less value than those applied to other phases. If that represents your thinking, you're in good company. Soldiers and politicians alike have typically failed to do endgame planning for wars; the predictable result has been more wars, more destruction—and, frequently, unbearable costs.

In the world of business, every campaign, every product, every service, and, indeed, every organization has a finite existence. Yet

168 JOHN A WARDEN III AND LELAND A. RUSSELL

few organizations take the time to plan the endgame, despite ample evidence that it is critically important.

American railroads, once the investment of choice for widows and orphans, assumed their business would go on forever. It didn't, and many an orphan and widow suffered from the railroads' no-endgame mistake.

It is human nature to avoid endgame planning. There is far more fulfillment in launching a project or product than there is in terminating one. Moreover, nobody likes to think about ending something that has been successful—especially when they feel a sense of ownership. So the natural tendency is to prolong it as long is possible. Even when a project or product is problematic, people will go to extraordinary lengths to continue it because of the uncertainty (and fear) about what comes next. Perhaps there's also an even deeper issue: Planning the endgame reminds us of our own mortality, which we spend most of our lifetime rejecting.

The result of not facing the reality of inevitable endings is often painful. We've seen it many times with beloved sports figures. You may recall the poignant story of the legendary slugger Babe Ruth. Instead of bowing out in glory at the top of his career, he hung in far beyond his prime until the New York Yankees finally traded him to play out his last forlorn season with the lowly Boston Braves.

FINISH WITH FINESSE

To remain a perennial winner, you must *finish with finesse*. That's what comedian Jerry Seinfield did after a nine-season run, when he announced that his Emmy-winning TV show wouldn't be returning for a tenth season. At that time the *Seinfield* show had been described as "the most profitable single piece of entertainment in history"; the termination announcement sparked months of virtual mourning by fans, and widespread media accolades for the ensemble.

The cast members agreed wholeheartedly with the decision because they agreed with Seinfeld's rationale:

I just know from being onstage for years and years and years, there is one moment where you have to feel the audience is still having a great time, and if you get off right there, they walk out of the theater excited. And yet, if you wait a little bit longer and try to give them more for their money, they walk out feeling not as good. If I get off now I have a chance at a standing ovation. That is what you go for.

Look at Dan Marino, one of the greatest passing quarterbacks in pro football history. He had an extraordinary career with the Miami Dolphins until, because of bad knees and age, he had a mediocre season in 1999. Would it have made more sense to stay and hope things got better, or to move on to other opportunities and leave his superb record untarnished? He faced the fact that his success cycle had peaked, and left the game in style.

Good investment-fund managers also know how to finish with finesse. Before a stock is purchased they have a plan to sell it and move on to the next deal when certain criteria have been met. Not surprisingly, the fund managers with the best-defined exit strategies are often the most successful.

But these are the exceptions. In our work with many different kinds of organizations, we've found that most people abhor the idea of abandoning a familiar product or service or, most emphatically, an organization, even when it is *not* successful. The termination process then becomes one of "finish with duress"—people hang on and on, until the handwriting is not only on the wall but on the floor and ceiling as well.

Think about the case of the Ford Motor Company and its Model T. The company was wildly successful with a very reliable, inexpensive car that met the basic needs of a country entering the automobile age. There were no frills and choices—as was said at the time, you could choose any color as long as it was black. Ford had a great car and a great business model.

But World War I changed it all. After the war, the creation of wealth exploded; everyone was making more money than ever.

Suddenly there were extra funds for amenities and those extra funds began to flow rapidly to General Motors, which under its CEO, Alfred Sloan, was providing multiple car models, options, and colors. In less than a decade, Ford's share of the market fell from over 50 percent to less than 30 percent and the company was on the verge of disaster. The problem: Ford had no endgame for the Model T.

Here, too, Prometheus offers a proven method.

DEFINING EXIT POINTS

In the Prometheus Process, you define Exit Points in advance. Without Exit Points, we inevitably find ourselves fighting desperate battles to save something that is no longer relevant. Because we hate to give up anything, we'll go to extraordinary lengths to continue on a course that was fine yesterday but is no longer germane. On the other hand, if we define Exit Points in advance, everyone is much more comfortable with the exit process because they know it will be done with style, and because they know it will free up energy to do something more profitable and exciting.

So, plan early. At the beginning of your campaign, define the criteria for the *Exit Point*—that moment in time beyond which you will experience diminishing returns.

Well-defined criteria for an Exit Point will help you:

- **Maximize (and retain) your financial gains** by ensuring that you exit at the right time. It is possible, for example, to squander all of your gains from a once-profitable product or service in a fruitless attempt to revive something that's in terminal collapse. This is the phenomenon known as "snatching defeat out of the jaws of victory."
- **Minimize your losses by "failing fast."** The Exit Point criteria will help you recognize when something isn't working. It provides a rational way to terminate failures quickly and decisively while the cost of failure is still relatively low. Without such Exit

Point criteria, you could be seduced by the "sunk-cost trap" that allows failures to drag on and on because you don't want to lose what has been invested.

- **End the game while you are strong.** The right Exit Point will leave you in the strongest possible position—not only financially, but psychologically—to launch your next effort.

If you don't define the Exit Point criteria early on, you have no formal way of evaluating when the end is near. Even if you do recognize it, the natural human tendency to "give it just one more chance" will take over.

In the business world, winners tend to get out while the "getting is good." How do they know when that moment arrives? There are several signals of the Exit Point for a product, service, or organization:

- Valuation Zenith
- Declining Financial Returns
- Market Shifts

EXIT POINT: VALUATION ZENITH

One way to define Exit Points is to find the point of maximum value of a product, process, or organization (which could be an entire company or a division of one). Think in terms of total value: not just the revenue being generated, but what you might realize from selling the product, process, or organization—or, as a worst-case measure, simply abandoning it.

Products and services tend to follow a fairly predictable curve. In the familiar pattern depicted in Figure 13.1, the left-hand side represents growing acceptance and sales following the birth of the product, the center part its biggest volume (and sometimes biggest profit), and the right side the decline in interest and sales.

When a product or service has reached the late stage of its success cycle—no longer "mature," but beginning to decline—this may be the time to activate your exit plan. Failure to do so may easily

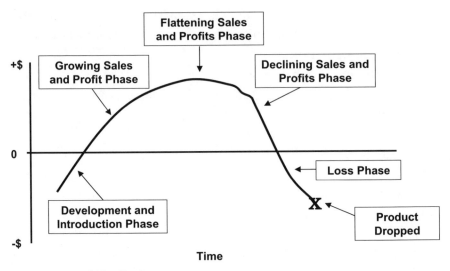

Figure 13.1 Life Cycles

mean that you will end up losing as much money on the product in its terminal stage as you made in its growth phase. Not only will you lose money, but you'll also waste management's time—an increasingly scarce resource—on something that has simply reached the end of the road. How much better it would be to have expensive talent focusing on the replacement product that may lead to better sales and profits.

How do you know when you are approaching that stage? If you wait for the numbers to decline, you may miss the Exit Point. So, rather than relying on lagging indicators, like year-end financials, focus on *leading* indicators like demographics, market trends, and innovations.

If, for example, you are continually monitoring the market, you will notice when the demographics of your customer base begin to shift or when emerging trends start to reduce the appeal of your product or service. This kind of early-warning system will alert you to new products and services that are gaining sales by offering more, different, or better features.

You should also look "upstream" at new innovations that could pose a strategic threat to you in the future. The manufacturers of magnetic computer storage tape, once a medium of choice, found themselves in this position at the time hard disks started to appear.

The first hard disks had much less capacity and were expensive, but if you watched their development for a short period, you would have noticed that they were rapidly moving upmarket and had the potential to put magnetic-tape makers out of business.

Other forces besides technology can also foreshadow the end-of-success cycle—geopolitics, for instance. Although the Berlin Wall fell in 1989, at that time most defense companies didn't come to grips with the fact that the boom era for defense was ending.

They got their wake-up call in September 1993, when Deputy Secretary of Defense Bill Perry called together the heads of the country's major aerospace companies for a meeting dubbed "the Last Supper." Perry told the assembled CEOs that the following year many of them would not be in business, that there were no longer enough defense dollars to sustain all the companies, and that some would have to merge or exit the business entirely.

His words kicked off the biggest merger spree in the history of the defense industry, with participants jockeying to remain competitive in a rapidly shrinking market. The resulting $100 billion in mergers reduced the number of major defense firms from fifty to five. Heeding the life-cycle signs earlier would have allowed some of the companies to better control their own destinies.

In addition to getting out toward the end of a life-cycle curve, it is sometimes possible, and sometimes extraordinarily profitable, to control the cycle instead of reacting to it. The Walt Disney Company for much of its existence periodically withdrew and reissued its classic animations, like *Snow White and the Seven Dwarfs*; Disney was deliberately controlling the market.

The most spectacular example, however, is Intel Corporation. Intel has dominated the central-processor chip market for nearly two decades by introducing new high-value, high-margin chips at an accelerating pace. As cloners begin to mimic the Intel product, Intel begins the exit process by slashing the price on the current model and simultaneously introducing a new high-margin product. With this deliberate termination process, Intel remains in charge of the market and always has an in-demand product for which it can charge premium prices.

EXIT POINT: DECLINING RETURNS

Financial returns are another obvious signal for exiting a product, service, or organization. If they are declining and the cause is strategic, such as intensifying competition that is permanently reducing margins to unacceptable levels, it may be time to exit and move to a higher-margin product.

Here we use margins in a broad sense; you can clearly make money on a product with low individual margins if you can sell enough units. However, you should predetermine your acceptable margins and volume levels; then, if a product or service starts slipping below that, you will know it is time to exit.

A caution: Don't get stuck in the "sunk-cost trap," where you count all the money you've put into a product or service and refuse to consider exiting until you have recouped it all. If you're in a downward spiral, exit regardless of past investments of time, energy, money, or emotions. Sunk costs are lost and sometimes holding on longer will only increase the loss, while also siphoning off capital and energy away from other opportunities.

Getting out doesn't mean you can't salvage anything. One man's junk *can* be another man's treasure. In fact, one of our clients had a product and an organization that no longer made strategic sense and was regularly (though not always) losing money. The company decided to get out by selling and soon found an organization that thought it knew how to make money with the product. Our client sold, and used the money and the saved management energy to concentrate on its high-value products. Everyone was happy.

You might argue that while a sale like this makes sense, the same doesn't apply when you abandon something, because abandoning brings no return. Not true: Maintenance of anything carries an expense, and by definition that expense represents an opportunity cost, which includes management time and energy. Could you invest the maintenance costs going to support a late-stage product, service, or organization into something that would have a higher future payoff? If so, what rationale stands in the way of a rapid and decisive exit?

EXIT POINT: MARKET SHIFTS

One of our clients was a nonprofit organization whose membership was made up exclusively of military veterans and whose single focus was on one class of injuries. As we helped this group to begin thinking strategically about its future, two stark facts emerged: The number of veterans with this type of injury was declining rapidly, and advances in treatment suggested that the total potential population with this injury would probably decline even more dramatically in the future. In a sense, the organization had won and had served its purpose well.

The first inclination of management, when faced with the realities of change, was to figure out how to perpetuate itself. As we moved further into the process, however, it became clear that perpetuation would mean a dramatic change in the organization's membership, leadership, and culture. The options, thus, were two: Exit on top with style, or become part of something that no one particularly wanted.

Their decision? The jury is still out. The rate of external change gave the group several years of financial security during which it could make a crucial decision. This organization, however, did what few do: It consciously addressed the option of closing shop and moving on.

Another market change example: Many years ago, pizza was a specialty item available only in a handful of restaurants. Few Americans ate pizza on a regular basis. People weren't familiar with this "exotic" food, and quality varied from restaurant to restaurant. There was no true national pizza market.

Then good, quality pizza started becoming available on a widespread basis.

As advertising and word of mouth spread information about this new lunch or dinner alternative, more and more Americans tried it and liked it. Soon the market had exceeded the critical mass needed to fuel self-sustaining rapid expansion.

The first mover had a real advantage. But because the potential market energy was so large (many customers, much money, many product types), it was possible for second movers to get in on the action—which, of course, further expanded the market as it became easier and cheaper to get a good pizza.

Times were good in the business. By and by, however, almost all Americans who might enjoy pizza were already pizza customers. The market began to stagnate.

At this point, the producers all think they must fight for a share of a fixed energy market, and prices and margins fall. The pizza business, for example, becomes commoditized and unexciting for investors and for innovative managers. At some point (tomorrow or the next day), tastes will change and the market will actually shrink, leading to further collapse in the value of pizza businesses.

From the standpoint of an investor, director, manager, and employee, the highest-value Exit Point was just before the stagnation period began.

Leaders and managers of most businesses are smart people who make many astute decisions and are not ignorant of what's going on around them. So, how is that smart people don't respond very well to signals saying that it is time to get out?

In large part, it is because endgame planning isn't widely taught, discussed, or understood. It's also because of a "can-do" attitude that often equates withdrawal with failure.

One additional factor, however, comes into play: "product fixation," the business equivalent of target fixation in the fighter pilot world. When you become so intent on hitting your target that the target is all you see, you lose awareness of what is going on around you. Many fighter pilots have crashed on a dive-bombing run because they became so fixated on hitting the target that they lost awareness of their altitude above the ground. When they finally did become aware, it was too late; there was insufficient altitude to pull out of their dive.

Exactly the same thing happens to a company desperately trying to save a dying product. All attention, all energy focuses on the rescue attempt; there is no perception that the external environment has changed to the point that the product no longer makes sense, or that an early pullout means being able to attack something else with a much higher chance of success—and a much lower chance of ending all chances!

Of course, when managers establish predefined Exit Points understood by all concerned, the probability of fatal product fixation decreases markedly.

EXIT ON TOP WITH STYLE

Exiting on top with style means that you do not leave money on the table unnecessarily and that you suitably reward all the people who contributed to reaching a successful end point. This concept becomes clearer when we flesh it out with details.

Success is a cycle. How you manage the ending stage of that cycle is just as important as how you manage the beginning and the middle stages.

Since "all's well that ends well," there should be a formal plan to finish with finesse. That means laying out what you will do when you have achieved your objectives. This plan answers some key questions: How will you know when it is time to exit? What steps must be taken to close down the current operations? How will you maintain our gains and avoid backsliding?

An important aspect of managing the ending is ensuring that you have adequate resources to properly close down the current operation. You should be prepared for the unexpected, because there is the potential for chaos and unpredictability at the end.

One other consideration: maintaining energy and enthusiasm to begin something new. The finale should include rewards and recognition for those who have contributed to reaching a successful end point.

The finale should also be both fun and memorable. The movie industry does this very well. When a picture is finished, the producer throws a crew party for the group that's been working together intensely for weeks or months. The participants leave the project on a high note, ready to begin another production with enthusiasm.

Whenever you're managing the ending of the project, don't forget the celebration, your own version of the crew party.

Chapter Debrief: **The Endgame**

Every campaign, every product, every service and, indeed, every organization has a finite existence.

People tend to avoid end-game planning for two reasons: 1) There is more fulfillment in launching a project or product than there is in terminating one; and 2) there is uncertainty and fear about what comes next.

To remain a perennial winner, you must finish with finesse. This means two things:

- Define the criteria for the Exit Point—that moment beyond which you will experience diminishing returns—early on.
- Exit on top with style; that is, don't leave money on the table unnecessarily and suitably reward all the people who contributed to reaching a successful end point.

There are several signals of the Exit Point for exiting a product, service, or organization:

- Valuation Zenith
- Declining Financial Returns
- Market Shifts

14

Cardinal Rules

> "It's sad to fail because of ignorance of how others have succeeded."

As we have seen, winning is not reacting to change, or guessing what might happen tomorrow and adapting to it. Winning is deciding what you want tomorrow to be and aggressively making it happen—creating your future.

And as we have also seen, the Prometheus Process offers you a system for winning: Build a blueprint of the future you want to create. Design an attack plan to get there. Campaign in parallel. Exit on top.

You now understand the flow. As you carry out the process, these Cardinal Rules will keep you on track and greatly increase your likelihood of winning.

"Think Like an Architect—Not Like a Bricklayer"

An architect thinks in top-down fashion—beginning with a grand concept of what the building should look like, and eventually dealing with the nitty-gritty of window size and placement, where the air-conditioning system will be located, where the electrical outlets will be, how plumbing pipes will run.

In business, top-down thinking is a necessity, if for no other reason than that bottom-up thinking is impossibly slow and inefficient because of the nearly infinite number of facts or bits of data on any given subject.

A true bottom-up approach would require careful examination of every fact directly or indirectly related to the problem. To gather and examine an infinite number of facts requires an infinity of time, something we are not likely to have available anytime soon.

So people take shortcuts, grabbing a few facts that are lying on the table or are otherwise easily available. With a tiny fraction of the facts relevant to the situation, they attempt to formulate large answers. Senior managers, intuitively understanding that not enough facts were used to make the integration process succeed, try to ease their concern by asking for more facts—which of course their subordinates dutifully set out to obtain. The result: more time wasted and little chance that additional bits of data will really improve what was a flawed process from the start.

Top-down thinking, in contrast, relies on an architectural, deductive approach. In this case, we start off with a broad understanding of the system in which we're operating, then differentiate down to find the small number of facts that are relevant to the problem.

More specifically, we start with an understanding of the *pattern* of the system, and then we look for matches or mismatches. Human beings are extraordinarily good at pattern recognition, so finding matches and mismatches rapidly leads to useful data and answers. (Conversely, we're terrible about finding meaning in quantities of raw data, which is why we like to convert large spreadsheets into graphical representations.)

Execute "Good Enough" Plans

"Audacious ignorance hath done the job while timorous wisdom stands debating." This axiom is as valid today as it was when written centuries ago. Create a plan that is "good enough," and execute it *now*. Improve as you move.

Many people have a problem with this. They loathe taking action until they are absolutely sure they haven't overlooked anything. Like engineers, they are susceptible to the urge to get one more data point in order to know with certainty the slope of a curve. The problem, of course, is that there is always an infinite amount of information available. And the longer you plan, the more your information grows stale and needs to be updated.

While you are gathering more and more information to create the perfect plan, someone else is gaining first-mover advantage. That is why a good enough plan rapidly executed is far superior to a perfect plan long delayed.

Take the Offensive

In a competitive situation, what should you do if you are unsure about the right action to take? The Prussians, who were the benchmark for military excellence for almost a century, concluded, "When in doubt, attack." This may sound like a wild, gunslinger approach, but the concept behind it—always take the offensive—is sound.

When you take the offensive, you have the opportunity to achieve exactly what you want because you set the agenda and the timetable. Assume, for example, that two competitors face each other in momentary limbo. Each one is trying to decide what to do and wondering what the other might do. The competitor that moves first gains the advantage and has the opportunity to achieve exactly what he or she want. The opponent's planning, on the other hand, is by necessity reactive. Moreover, the opponent's response options are limited and *simply not losing becomes the best possible outcome.*

Taking the offensive in business means more, however, than simply making the first move in a competitive situation. It means going after profit growth by innovating, launching new products, and opening new markets. This kind of proactive approach— aggressively attacking to drive continuing profit growth—is very different from the reactive approach, in which you try to maintain status quo profitability through defensive measures like cost reduction and price cutting.

Plan to Win: Impose Your Plan

Businesses and military strategists alike rarely take the time to plan beyond the first few steps because they believe "No plan ever survives the first contact with the enemy." They simply decide upon their first move, after which their "plan" is to sit back and see what happens. For all practical purposes, they turn over responsibility for the future to the market or to their opponent. In fact, most plans that fail do so because the planners deliberately cede the initiative and become reactive.

If you truly want to succeed, you must *plan to win* and then *impose your plan.*

That was the secret to success in the Desert Storm air campaign. The Checkmate team designed a plan to win: a strategy that would immediately seize the initiative and then maintain momentum, never giving the opponent (the Iraqi system) sufficient time to regain its balance.

Equally important, the execution of the plan was not tentative. The coalition forces imposed the plan on Iraq by aggressively and repeatedly attacking its Centers of Gravity using a fast, precise, parallel approach.

There should be nothing tentative, nothing hesitant about your planning or your execution. Like the leaders of Desert Storm, strike quickly and decisively.

Don't Underestimate What It Takes to Win

This Cardinal Rule requires careful estimation of the cost of participating at a sufficient level to succeed. If you drive people into a corner where their very survival is at stake, they will give their all to survive.

If you want to compete, you need to be willing to pay enough to win.

Competitors rarely have the same level of interest in the outcome of a competition. For a small company with a successful product, the arrival of a new competitor is potentially life-threatening. The smaller firm typically reacts by trying to improve the product, cut prices, and generally do whatever it takes to prevent the new competitor from succeeding. Since it is fighting for its survival, its response knows few bounds.

In contrast, it is not uncommon for a large company to enter a market by "testing the waters." If the test succeeds, the company will increase its efforts; if not, it simply pulls the plug.

What is wrong with this approach? If the competitors are committed, it will probably fail. A market that appeared to offer easy opportunity suddenly becomes very tough. The competition reacts, expected sales fail to materialize, and headquarters soon decides the effort was an error.

As you look at new initiatives for your company, answer this question: Who is most committed to winning, you or your competition? If the answer is your competition, reconsider the initiative. In short, don't underestimate what it takes to win; if you are not willing to pay the price of success, don't play.

Choose Enemies and Friends

There is a certain tendency to think that a higher authority designates enemies and friends and that there is not much we can do about it. But the fact is, there is almost always a choice.

Microsoft, for instance, is an outstanding organization, but over time it made a number of enemies because of what many perceived as arrogance and overly aggressive business practices. So, when the Justice Department launched its antitrust suit against Microsoft, it had no problem finding witnesses willing to testify. Few prominent people came forward for the defense.

Had Microsoft not created so many enemies, the Justice Department might never have been able to develop and prosecute its case.

Think of all the energy and money Microsoft spent trying to defend itself because the company had so gratuitously offended so many people.

An opposite case in point involves Jamaica Hospital Medical Center in Queens, New York, which a few years back was in dire financial straits. Fortunately, the state of New York agreed to help with a bond issue that allowed the Center to recover, expand, and provide more and better service to its community. A major reason for this support was that, through the preceding ten years, Jamaica's leaders had made it a point to visit key government officials at the state capital in Albany, not to ask for anything but simply to say hello and keep them informed of the health-care needs of the community. Not surprisingly, when Jamaica needed help, there were many sympathetic friends in Albany who were ready to lend a hand in finding a solution.

The strategic lesson here is simple: Friends are good and you cannot have too many; if you have enemies, figure out what it will take to turn them into friends and pursue the effort.

Use an Indirect Approach

Strategy can be approached directly, or it can be approached indirectly.

The direct attack is like a prizefighter deliberately exchanging blows toe-to-toe with his opponent. Assuming the opponents are roughly equal in strength, size, and skill, the outcome may essentially depend on who can absorb the most punishment.

The direct attack always generates the greatest amount of opposition and creates the most enemies. So why do most people use it? Simply because few are in the habit of taking the time to think through their strategic options. Since the direct attack is obvious, it is easy to plan and execute. A machismo factor also comes into play; it seems like the "manly" thing to do.

If you have limited time and resources, and care about the cost of winning, you are far better off with the indirect attack. With this approach, *you do not appear to be doing anything,* yet you are actually planning and executing something subtle and unexpected.

What is an indirect attack? Recall how the Japanese automobile makers succeeded in penetrating the American market: not with a direct attack against the existing market leaders, but by introducing small cars for which Detroit thought there was no market or profit. By the time Detroit realized its error, the Japanese held key market Centers of Gravity and were ready to move into the higher-margin large-car market. The indirect attack had succeeded.

The indirect approach may take more thinking and more careful preparation, but it is safer and far more effective. And, if it doesn't work, at least you are not locked into a costly slugging match.

Stay Out of the Balkans

The "Balkans" is a metaphor for activities and projects that don't help you achieve your Future Picture.

The term stems from Germany's ill-fated decision to conquer the Balkans during World War II, which required diverting nearly a million men from the German campaign against the Russians. But the Balkans were not strategically important to Germany, and the useless effort undoubtedly contributed to its defeat.

Many organizations—or more likely *most*—are much like the Germans: They involve themselves in operations that are not strategically important, and in the process either lose strategically important contests or fail to do as well as they could.

Think about it: If the Germans had defeated the Balkan countries in months, would they have won World War II? Conversely, if they had been beaten in the Balkans or had never gone there, would they have lost the war? The answer to both questions is clearly no. Yet to the German troop commanders throughout the war, operating in the Balkans seemed proper and essential. It was up to headquarters to recognize where strategic opportunity and risk lay. Too many times, we are like those troop commanders and become mesmerized by projects or operations that in themselves are fine, but that have no true connection to the strategic aims of the organization.

Every organization, including yours, has its own "Balkans." They become very apparent once you paint your Future Picture. Suddenly you see that some existing activities and projects that may be good in themselves are not really moving you toward your long-term success. In fact, they are actually retarding it by absorbing valuable time and resources.

Spend some time identifying the projects that don't have any real connection with the strategic objectives of your company. The first step in withdrawing from these projects is recognizing them for what they are—bringing some benefits, perhaps, and with good people working very hard on them, but simply not relevant when measured against your organization's strategy and resources.

Stay out of the Balkans! (And if you are already in them, get out!)

Exploit Your "Key Force"

Every organization has "forces"—groups of people organized according to the kind of job they do or the product for which they have responsibility. The military, for example, has air, land, and sea forces. Each of these groups is competent and justifiably proud of its contribution. Not surprisingly, they are equally eager to participate in every combat operation. So, to "keep peace in the family," war plans are often designed in a way that ensures all branches of the military have a prominent role.

Should all the forces participate in every conflict? Do they all have equal value in every phase of a conflict? Usually not. Someone must decide which group is most important at a given time and designate them as the "Key Force."

General Schwarzkopf did a masterful job of this during Desert Storm. Airpower was the designated Key Force until the Iraqis were sufficiently paralyzed and unable to offer serious resistance to the ground forces. But the general had to hold back Army and Marine forces pushing to get into the fight. Had he not done so, the human cost of the war would have been significantly greater.

What are the "forces" in a business organization? They include R&D, manufacturing, marketing, and finance groups, to name a few. Just as in the military, a problem of role-priority arises. Unless they are strategically enlightened, the vice president of Division A automatically expects a "fair share" of the budget, even in a situation where Division B is in a position to do the most to further the long-term aims of the company.

If your objective is to win as quickly and cheaply as possible, select the group or groups that can best advance your strategic objectives at a given time. Declare them to be the current Key Force(s). Then give them the opportunity and resources to do what needs to be done.

Maintain and Use Reserves

We are all familiar with the use of "reserves" in a military campaign—resources that are deliberately withheld until there is a critical juncture in a campaign. Military commanders understand the value and necessity of maintaining reserves to meet unexpected situations—both setbacks and opportunities.

In 1940, the Germans conducted an intense air campaign against Britain using all of their available resources. The British, although in mortal peril, deliberately held back almost a quarter of their pilots and aircraft. When the German pilots were nearing exhaustion and believed that their opponent was on the ropes, the British fully committed their reserves. Imagine the Germans' shock when suddenly confronted with a far larger number of planes than they had previously seen. The German air force at that point had no reserves; the very next day, the Germans called off their long-planned invasion of Britain.

The lessons: Timing is important. And reserves should be used at a moment when they can have the greatest impact.

You can magnify the effect of your decisions, not just by when but also *how* your reserves are deployed. The piecemeal approach is usually ineffective: Deploying reserves en masse often makes a critical difference. If you have an advertising budget in reserve, and parcel it out over the course of a year by running an occasional ad in a newspaper or magazine, you are not likely to have a significant impact. But put it all into a series of high-impact ads at the exact right moment, and you may fundamentally change the situation.

Except in a financial sense, the concept of reserves is relatively unknown in the business world. In fact, the prevailing wisdom is that every available resource should be used to the maximum. Moreover, the explicit focus of cost cutting—a defensive tactic—is to eliminate anything that is not fully employed in delivering immediate value. As the organization's resources are cut to the bone, there is little or no consideration for the strategic consequences.

If an organization truly wants to win, it needs leaders and managers who understand the value of maintaining reserves and are willing to commit them, to reinforce success or to check failure.

Focus on the Future

All too often, people waste valuable time analyzing and debating what happened yesterday, or defending past decisions and business practices.

Rather than looking in the rearview mirror, they would be better served by looking through the windshield, which happens to be about thirty times larger than the rearview mirror for a very good reason. It is far more important to know where you are going than to know where you have been.

Since there is no way to change the past, let go of it and concentrate your creative energy on achieving the Future Picture.

You can help people focus forward by:

• Including everyone in the design of the future. The more hearts and minds you engage in this process, the better.

- Introducing a new vocabulary that causes people to think about tomorrow. There is enormous power in using future-focused phrases like "Scope the Environment," "Paint the Future," and "Engrave the Guiding Precepts." They cause people to look through the windshield at the road ahead, rather than in the rearview mirror.

Maintain Momentum—Bypass Obstacles

Maintain momentum! When you begin executing your plan (as well as during the planning process itself), you'll encounter obstacles—some things won't work the way you anticipated. In the old serial world, an obstacle was likely to force a halt while you tried to overcome it; in the new parallel world, obstacles are there to bypass. Your objective is to maintain momentum and win quickly before the system can counter your efforts. You must overcome the normal reaction, which is to fix everything before you proceed; instead, when confronted with an obstacle, you will simply bypass it and move on. You'll be amazed at how many of the obstacles thought to be barriers to success will turn out to be irrelevant.

You will, of course, find many people who are uncomfortable with the idea of leaving unsolved problems behind. Encourage them by emphasizing the need for high velocity and for producing system effects. Parallel operations can afford to have some aspects not work well. Keep moving! Go for *velocity!*

When and where do you use these Cardinal Rules? Use them throughout the Prometheus Process. Apply them at every level of your organization. The higher the number of people who understand and use the Cardinal Rules, the more effective your organization will be. When you begin to hear junior people using a phrase like "we are in the Balkans," don't be surprised. Be delighted . . . and know that your organization is now beginning to think and act strategically in all its components.

You now know the four imperatives of the Prometheus

Process—*Design the Future, Target for Success, Campaign to Win,* and *Finish with Finesse.* Follow them and apply the Cardinal Rules and your odds of success will increase dramatically.

Chapter Debrief: Cardinal Rules

To increase your probability of success, follow the Cardinal Rules of Prometheus:

- Think like an architect.
- Execute good enough plans.
- Take the offensive.
- Impose your plan.
- Do not underestimate what it takes to win.
- Choose enemies and friends.
- Use an indirect approach.
- Stay out of the Balkans.
- Exploit your Key Force.
- Maintain and use reserves.
- Focus on the future.
- Bypass obstacles.
- Maintain momentum.

15

Prometheus @ Work

"Knowledge won't keep. It must be applied."

Winning organizations assimilate new knowledge quickly. They also recognize that knowledge is of little value until it is profitably applied. That is why, when someone at any level discovers something that will help build a better product or improve a process or create a more elegant business model, the organization rapidly translates it into practical use.

We've now shown you the Prometheus approach to winning in a warp-speed world. At this point you have enough knowledge of Prometheus to get started. Our hope is that you will put this knowledge to work immediately.

As you do so, follow the Prometheus Process:

Design Your Future

Scope the broad business, economic, and political environment in which you will be operating. By doing so, you will come to understand the opportunities that may be available to you, the obstacles you may encounter, and the trends you will not want to buck unknowingly.

Paint a Future Picture that is clear and truly compelling. This is the beacon by which everyone involved will guide their progress; it's vitally important that everyone understand what that picture is and what it means for them.

Engrave the Guiding Precepts for your organization. Because these behavioral ground rules reflect your organization's essence and its character, take them seriously. Do not create a Guiding Precept you don't believe in and are not willing to enforce.

Establish Measures of Merit that will tell you whether you are on the right track strategically. Associate these high-level measures directly to elements of your Future Picture and ensure that their focus is strategic, not tactical.

Target for Success

"Map" the systems in which you will be operating. Always begin with the largest systems you can reasonably manage and then work down to subsystems as necessary. Identify the key Centers of Gravity in those systems that will need to be affected for the system to match your Future Picture.

Determine the Desired Effects for each Center of Gravity and how you will measure your success in achieving them. Ensure that every effect relates directly to realizing your desired future.

Campaign to Win

Commission parallel campaigns that have a laserlike focus on getting measurable results as rapidly as possible. Remember, when multiple campaigns with the same strategic intent operate in parallel, their velocity and impact increase considerably.

Organize for success, not for bureaucratic or political convenience. Create an organizational structure that will support, rather than hinder, the success of your campaigns.

Finish with Finesse

Define in advance the criteria for your Exit Point—that moment in time beyond which you will experience diminishing returns. This will ensure that you maximize and retain your financial gains, that you will be able to quickly recognize when something is not working, and that you end the game in a manner that leaves you in the strongest possible position to launch your next effort—not only financially, but psychologically.

Lay out a plan for what you will do when you have achieved your strategic objectives. Answer some key questions: How will you know when it is time to exit? What steps must be taken to close down the current operations? How will you maintain your gains and avoid backsliding?

APPLYING PROMETHEUS

A central theme of *Winning in FastTime* is that it's for the *whole* organization. Use Prometheus at every level. You will find enormous power in having a shared process and vocabulary that allows people to think together, and to communicate across disciplines and organizational lines about strategic issues.

Ted Nagengast, one of the Prometheus leaders at McDonald's, noted what he considered a remarkable thing about the process: You can use any part of it and have an immediate, positive impact. For example, another one of our clients, after only one Prometheus briefing, decided to use the Open Planning approach in its annual budgeting process. Within a few days, all of the managers had been gathered together in one room at the same time to work through the budget allocations.

They found that this approach had three immediate benefits. First, it reduced the budgeting-process time by half. Second, because decisions were made in the open, everyone felt good about them and supported them. When funds were shifted from one department to another, almost everyone supported the decision.

Third, the approach created momentum that signaled to the rest of the organization that it would no longer be business as usual.

Another client observed that having a large number of people at all levels of the organization learning Prometheus together allowed them to apply the concepts quickly, even before everyone understood all of them.

Developing expertise in anything takes time. But knowledge comes from "action learning"—applying the Prometheus concepts to real-world situations. It's through such practical application that people become individually proficient in Prometheus.

Competency evolves into expertise naturally. People no longer think about individual process steps or following rules by rote. They move into what one client called a "flow state" in which they are doing many things elegantly, simultaneously, and unconsciously.

A middle manager in a large organization explained her experience this way:

> When I first learned the concepts, some of them made immediate sense. Others, like Centers of Gravity, I did not fully grasp. But as soon as I began to map the Centers of Gravity in my own department, everything came together. You might say that the proverbial lightbulb went off. Suddenly, I began to "see the system" and became excited about "orchestrating" parallel operations to change it.
>
> In retrospect, it's somewhat like learning to drive a car. While it may seem a little bit awkward at first, it soon becomes second nature. For example, the other day I identified a new Center of Gravity. The very first question I asked myself was, "What's the Desired Effect?" The next day I brought my staff together in an Open Planning session and we used the Five Rings model to map the Center of Gravity and create an action plan. It took less than one hour.

BREAKING THE ELASTIC LIMIT

All of our clients agree on one thing: Prometheus calls for new ways of doing business. They also agree that, without firm leadership at the top, it's very easy to fall back into the way you normally do things.

When you're in the process of embedding the Prometheus approach into the genetic code of an organization, there can initially be stubborn resistance. Leadership is essential to overcoming that resistance. Denny Donahue, the Prometheus Orchestrator at The Bama Companies, strongly emphasizes this point:

> The leader's job is to push the organization past its elastic limit. That means taking the status quo off the table and questioning any activity that isn't in consonance with Prometheus. Every time someone comes up with a reason to go back to the normal way of doing things, the message should be, "This is the way we are going to do business, so get used to it." Reinforcing this message is important because you want everyone, or at least a critical mass, to rapidly embrace the mindset and apply the process.

How long is such firm leadership necessary? It must be maintained until the entire organization (the system) is moving in the desired direction. Otherwise the elastic limit isn't going to be broken. Prometheus will end up being just another "flavor of the month."

DEMONSTRATING COMMITMENT

To "install" Prometheus in an organization, there must be a critical mass of committed people at multiple levels who understand and practice the techniques. That commitment begins at the top.

As one CEO said:

The leaders need to commit to becoming experts in Prometheus themselves. I realized that early on and made it a point to attend the educational sessions, do the homework, and learn everything I could. As CEO, I had to fully embrace the Prometheus approach and "walk the talk." I also had to assume personal responsibility for keeping it alive.

The same was true of my direct reports. They had to invest their time and energy into learning and integrating the principles into their own thinking and actions. All of this paid off. We were able to answer questions and make decisions in an aligned way. Most importantly, we modeled the new behaviors.

There are many other ways to demonstrate commitment. Establish a campaign room. Designate a Campaign Orchestrator. Create Rules of Engagement that free up people and funds to solve strategic problems and seize strategic opportunities.

LEARNING THE LANGUAGE

When we say that we know a language, we imply that we have a reasonable command of its lexicon, allowing us to communicate with others who know the language.

Woven into the Prometheus Imperatives and Cardinal Rules is a comprehensive lexicon for communicating about strategic issues that can be used at all levels of the organization. This lexicon includes not only the words and definitions themselves, but also visual representations of concepts, stories, and phrases and metaphors like Instant Thunder, "the Time Value of Action," "go to Rome," and "stay out of the Balkans."

This lexicon is specifically designed to be unique and memorable. There are many ways to reinforce the lexicon. One of our clients, for example, had Prometheus "dialogues" to ensure that everyone understood the terms and what they meant. Others have "gone visual," creating print media ranging from wall posters to wallet-size reminder cards. One client used flash cards and games to reinforce the concepts.

THINKING LIKE A WINNER

Finally, as you apply the Prometheus Process, remember the mindset that underlies its insight and power:

- *Win in FastTime*—Decide what you want your tomorrow to be, and then make it happen faster than the rate of change in your competitive environment.
- *Use Instant Thunder*—Remember the formula for winning in the twenty-first century: Think strategically, focus sharply, and move quickly.
- *Change the Game*—You won't win by following the rules of yesterday. Create your own rules with a winning strategy: an integrated plan that will take you from vision to execution to completion.
- *Focus on Centers of Gravity*—Everything happens within a system and every system has Centers of Gravity. Identify them and act on them rapidly and in parallel. This is the secret to rapid, decisive system change.

A FUTURE THOUGHT

Now the essential question remains: Will Prometheus work for you and your organization? It led to victory in the fiery tempest of the Desert Storm air campaign, and it has been proven on the twenty-first century battlefields of business. Organizations in a wide variety of industries—high-tech, entertainment, finance, health care, and food service, to name a few—have used the method and praised the results.

Our intention is for these Prometheus concepts to sharpen your thinking about how to design the future and then to confidently achieve it. Our fervent hope is that you will put Prometheus to work quickly so that you and your organization can become renowned for . . . Winning in *FastTime.*

Bibliography

CHAPTER 2: INSTANT THUNDER

Atkinson, Rick. *Crusade: The Untold Story of the Gulf War.* Boston: Houghton Mifflin Company, 1993.

Clancy, Tom. *Fighter Wing: A Guided Tour of an Air Force Combat Wing.* New York: Berkley Books, 1995.

Gordon, Michael R., and Bernard E. Trainor. *The Generals' War: The Inside Story of the Conflict in the Gulf.* Boston: Little, Brown and Company, 1995.

Hallion, Richard P. *Storm Over Iraq: Air Power and the Gulf War.* Washington, DC: Smithsonian Institution Press, 1997.

Palmer, Michael A. *Guardians of the Gulf: A History of America's Expanding Role in the Persian Gulf, 1833–1992.* New York: Free Press, 1992

Powell, Colin L., and Joseph E. Persico (Contributor). *My American Journey: An Autobiography.* New York: Random House, 1995.

Reynolds, Richard T. *Heart of the Storm.* Maxwell Air Force Base, AL: Air University Press, 1995.

Schwarzkopf, H. Norman, with Peter Petre. *It Doesn't Take a Hero.* New York: Bantam Books, 1992.

Smith, Perry M. *How CNN Fought the War: A View from the Inside.* New York: A Birch Lane Press Book, 1991.

CHAPTER 3: CHANGING THE GAME

Christensen, Clayton M. *The Innovator's Dilemma: When New Technologies Cause Great Firms to Fail.* Boston: Harvard Business School Press, 1997.

Dell, Michael. *Direct from Dell: Strategies That Revolutionized an Industry.* New York: HarperCollins, 1999.

Freiberg, Kevin, and Jackie Freiberg. *Nuts!: Southwest Airlines' Crazy Recipe for Business and Personal Success.* Austin, TX: Bard Press, 1996.

Hamel, Gary, and C. K. Prahalad. *Competing for the Future.* Boston: Harvard Business School Press, 1994.

"Signal Success," *Forbes,* March 22, 1999.

CHAPTER 4: CENTERS OF GRAVITY

Clausewitz, Carl von. *On War.* Translated and edited by Michael C.
    Howard and Peter Paret. Princeton, NJ: Princeton University
    Press, 1976.
Fuller, J.F.C. *The Generalship of Alexander the Great.* London: Eyre &
    Spottiswoode, 1958.
"Pokémon Fever Turns Into a Headache at Burger King," *Los
    Angeles Times,* November 12, 1999.
Sabbagh, Karl. *Twenty-First-Century Jet: The Making and Marketing of
    the Boeing 777.* New York: Simon & Schuster, 1995.
"Satellite Venture Will Go Down in Flames, Literally," *Los Angeles
    Times*, March 18, 2000.
"Schwab, Merrill Plan Blue Industry Lines," *Los Angeles Times,*
    November 28, 1999.
Senge, Peter M. *The Fifth Discipline: The Art and Practice of the
    Learning Organization.* New York: Doubleday/Currency, 1990.
"Studio Built Victory 'One Brick at a Time,'" *Los Angeles Times,*
    March 27, 2000.
Wallace, James, and Jim Erickson. *Hard Drive: Bill Gates and the
    Making of the Microsoft Empire.* New York: Wiley, 1992.

CHAPTER 5: THE ENVIRONMENT

Christensen, Clayton M. *The Innovator's Dilemma: When New
    Technologies Cause Great Firms to Fail.* Boston: Harvard Business
    School Press, 1997.
Dell, Michael. "Building the Infrastructure for Twenty-First-Century
    Commerce." Keynote Address, Las Vegas, NV: May 12, 1999.
Gates, William H. *Business at the Speed of Thought.* New York:
    Warner Books, 1999.
Gilder, George. *Gilder Technology Report.* Housatonic, MA: Gilder

Publishing and *Forbes,* 1998–2000.

————. *Microcosm.* New York: Simon & Schuster, 1989.

Groves, Andrew S. *Only the Paranoid Survive: How to Exploit the Crisis Points That Challenge Every Company and Career.* New York: Doubleday/Currency, 1996.

Harry, Mikel, and Richard Schroeder. *Six Sigma: The Breakthrough Management Strategy Revolutionizing the World's Top Corporations.* New York: Doubleday/Currency, 2000.

Kurzweil, Ray. *The Age of Spiritual Machines.* New York: Viking Penguin, 1999.

Moore, Geoffrey A. *Crossing the Chasm: Marketing and Selling High-Tech Products to Mainstream Customers.* New York: HarperCollins, 1991.

Toffler, Alvin, and Heidi Toffler. *War and Anti-War: Survival at the Dawn of the 21st Century.* Boston: Little, Brown and Company, 1993.

CHAPTER 6: THE FUTURE PICTURE

Aleinikov, Andrei. *Mega-Creator, from Creativity to Mega-, Giga-, and Infi-Creativity.* Midland, MI: Northwood University, The McKay Press, 2000

Altshuller, Genrich. *And Suddenly the Inventor Appeared: TRIZ, the Theory of Inventive Problem Solving.* Worcester, MA: Technical Innovation Center, 1994.

"An Eye on the Future," *Time,* December 27, 1999.

Kenney, Charles. *Riding the Runaway Horse: The Rise and Decline of Wang Laboratories.* Boston: Little, Brown and Company, 1992.

CHAPTER 7: GUIDING PRECEPTS

Collins, James C., and Jerry I. Porras. *Built to Last: Successful Habits of Visionary Companies.* New York: HarperBusiness, 1994.

Dell, Michael. *Direct from Dell: Strategies That Revolutionized an Industry.* New York: HarperCollins, 1999.

Farrago, Ladislas. *Patton: Ordeal and Triumph.* 2d ed. New York: Dell Publishing Company, Inc., 1970

Freiberg, Kevin, and Jackie Freiberg. *Nuts!: Southwest Airlines' Crazy Recipe for Business and Personal Success.* Austin, TX: Bard Press, 1996.

Fuller, J.F.C. *The Decisive Battles of the Western World and Their Influence Upon History.* Volume I. London: Eyre & Spottiswoode, 1963.

———. *The Second World War, 1939–45: A Statistical and Tactical History.* London: Eyre & Spottiswoode, 1948.

Jackson, Tim. *Inside Intel: Andy Grove and the Rise of the World's Most Powerful Chip Company.* New York: Dutton, 1997.

McDowell, Robert L., and William L. Simon. *Driving Digital: Microsoft and Its Customers Speak About Thriving in the eBusiness Era.* New York: HarperBusiness, 2001.

Smith, Perry M. *Rules and Tools for Leaders: A Down-to-Earth Guide to Effective Managing.* Garden City Park, NY: Avery Publishing Group, 1998.

CHAPTER 11: PARALLEL CAMPAIGNS

Dupuy, Trevor N. *A Genius for War: The German Army and General Staff, 1807–1945.* London: MacDonald and Jane's, 1977.

CHAPTER 12: ORGANIZING FOR SUCCESS

Christensen, Clayton M. *The Innovator's Dilemma: When New Technologies Cause Great Firms to Fail.* Boston: Harvard Business School Press, 1997.

"Inside Microsoft: The Untold Story of How the Internet Forced Bill Gates to Reverse Course," *Business Week,* July 15, 1996.

Luttwak, Edward N., and J. F. Gilliam. *The Grand Strategy of the Roman Empire: From the First Century A.D. to the Third.* Baltimore and London: Johns Hopkins University Press, 1976.

"Technophobia Still Affects Some Americans," *Wall Street Journal,* July 26, 1993.

CHAPTER 13: THE ENDGAME

Associated Press, "Marino Retires after 17 Seasons," March 15, 2000, as posted on *Sun-Sentinel* online, http://www.sun-sentinel.com/graphics/marino/athlete/injuries.html.

Fuller, J.F.C. *Decisive Battles of the Western World and Their Influence Upon History.* Volume III. London: Eyre & Spottiswoode, 1963.

Groves. Andrew S. *Only the Paranoid Survive: How to Exploit the Crisis Points That Challenge Every Company and Career.* New York: Doubleday/Currency, 1996.

"It's All about Timing," January 12, 1998, Vol. 151, No. 1, p. 2, as posted on *Time* online, http://www.time.com/time/magazine/1998/don/9801112/cover3.html

Korb, Lawrence J., "Defense Mega-Mergers Weaken the U.S.," *Newsday,* April 28, 1998, as posted on http://brookings.org/views/op-ed/korb/19980428.htm.

Peters, Tom. *Thriving on Chaos: Handbook for a Management Revolution.* New York: HarperCollins and Random House, 1987.

"Seinfeld Laughs All the Way to the Bank," September 8, 1998, as posted on *Time* online, http://www.time.com/time/daily/0,2960,14674,00.html.

Slywotzky, Adrian J., and David J. Morrison. *The Profit Zone: How Strategic Business Design Will Lead You to Tomorrow's Profits.* New York: Random House, 1997.

Sun-tzu. *The Art of War.* Translated and with an introduction by Samuel B. Griffith. London: Oxford University Press, 1963.

Taylor, Telford. *The Breaking Wave.* New York: Simon & Schuster, 1967.

Warden III, John A. *The Air Campaign: Planning for Combat.* Rev. ed. http:/www.iuniverse.com./marketplace/bookstore/:toExcel Press, 2000.

Acknowledgments

The development of what was to become the Prometheus Process started years ago; its specific intellectual roots owe much to Colonel (then Major) Roger B. Fox, my history instructor and mentor at the U.S. Air Force Academy, and to Dr. Frederick H. Hartmann, who, while on sabbatical from the U.S. Navy War College, became my professor of strategy and my thesis director at Texas Tech University.

Between these two men in my student days and the Gulf War are dozens more who helped me better understand strategy and how to make it happen despite the opposition. To those many, thank you!

The Gulf War was the first major testing ground for the core ideas in this book. They worked—although obviously, we would do a better job today given the lessons learned during and after the war. Thus, my greatest debt is to all those men and women who contributed to creating, refining, nurturing, protecting, and executing the air campaign. The following are a few of those with whom I had direct contact (with the exception of the President himself) and to whom I owe special appreciation:

Political

- President George Bush, who made good on his promise that "this aggression will not stand";
- Secretary of Defense Richard Cheney, who listened and acted decisively;
- Air Force Secretary Donald Rice, who championed airpower and the air campaign against major opposition;
- National Security Adviser Richard Haas, who adeptly combined the military and the political;
- Charles Allen, whose superb intelligence work and policy contributions may never be publicly recognized and rewarded;
- Dr. Edward N. Luttwak, who precipitated an extraordinary meeting in December 1990 of the President and his Joint Chiefs of Staff; and

206 JOHN A WARDEN III AND LELAND A. RUSSELL

- National Security staff member Lieutenant General (then Colonel) Michael Hayden, later head of the National Security Agency, who played an indispensable role in sychronizing Persian Gulf policy development and military operations.

Senior Military

- General Colin Powell, Chairman of the Joint Chiefs of Staff, who guided and oversaw every aspect of the war effort;
- General Norman Schwarzkopf, one of the twentieth century's top military commanders, who made it all happen brilliantly from start to finish;
- General Michael C. Dugan, Air Force Chief of Staff, who was willing to do what had to be done for his service and country;
- General John "Mike" Loh, Air Force Vice Chief of Staff, who launched and nurtured the planning effort through its most difficult periods;
- General Tony McPeak, Air Force Chief of Staff (General Dugan's successor), who supported the air campaign and who convincingly conveyed its potential and his confidence in it to the President on two crucial occasions;
- General (then Lieutenant General) Charles Horner, General Schwarzkopf's senior airman, who ably organized his forces and executed the air campaign; and
- Lieutenant General (then Major General) Minter Alexander, Director of Air Force plans, who spent many long nights with us in Checkmate and who fervently supported the air campaign effort.

The Air Campaign Planners

- Brigadier General (then Lieutenant Colonel) Dave Deptula, who played key planning and execution roles in Washington and in

Riyadh, was one of the three officers who accompanied me to Riyadh to deliver the plan to General Chuck Horner, and who stayed in Riyadh, where he was the "engine" of the theater planning effort;

- Colonel (then Lieutenant Colonel) Ben Harvey, who was part of the creation, helped bring to bear the resources of the whole intelligence community, and was one of the three officers who accompanied me on the trip to Riyadh;

- Colonel (then Lieutenant Colonel) Ronnie Stanfill, who was also there at the creation and who tirelessly pushed our thinking toward more and more precision, was the third of the officers who went with me to Riyadh;

- Major (then Captain) Dan Taylor, my Executive Officer, who kept me and the entire Checkmate operation supplied and moving;

- The late Chuck Kissel, Intelligence Officer, whose work was the stuff of legends; and

- The hundreds of other officers, enlisted personnel, and civilians who made huge contributions to every aspect of the planning process. The photograph shows some of them on the steps of the Pentagon in March 1991 after the successful conclusion of the war.

The Media

- Major General (Retired) Perry M. Smith, then CNN commentator, who gave nearly a billion people around the world accurate, real-time information on the war. His influence on policy makers was extraordinary.

The Fighters

- And most of all—to the men and women who executed Desert Storm so splendidly and ushered in a new era in warfare.

Some of the key Checkmate open planners at the river entrance of the Pentagon at the war's end: John Warden (center) and in alphabetical order: Ross Ashley, Judy Austin, Dale Autry, Jeff Barnett, Bill Behmyer, Jim Blackburn, Dan Bohlin, Ed Bondzeleski, Sylvia Branch, Charlotte Burlock, Butch Byrd, Sharon Claxton, Glenn Cobb, Bob Coffman, Steve Cullen, Dan Davies, Burnell Davis, Wayne Debban, Mable Dixon, Scott Dorff, Mike Dunn, Jerry Folkerts, Virginia Fromel, Mary Gambale, Bill Gast, Chris Guenther, Scott Hack, Ben Harvey, Leonard Heavner, Steve Hedger, Dale Hill, Chris Hines, Ralph Hitchens, Hans Hjertquist, Lee Horn, Al Howey, Mike Kayes, T. K. Kearney, Rich King, "Sky" King, Emery "Mike" Kiraly, Chuck Kissel, Frank Kistler, Dan Kolpin, Bert Lassiter, John Lawmaster, Dave Leeper, Bill Lipsmeyer, Jeff Lord, Bill Lucyshyn, Robert Massey, Mark Matthews, Jim McCormick, Phil Meilinger, Dick Moore, Mike Nelson, Terry New, Rich Noble, Brian Overington, James Patterson, Scott "Truck" Pelletier, Gregg Phillips, Steve Pitotti, Mike Reedy, Doctor Roddey, John Roe, Roy "Mac" Sikes, Tanker Snyder, Ronnie Stanfill, Steve "Sterno" Stern, Fred Strain, Bill Switzer, Dan Taylor, Tommy Thompson, Wayne Thompson, Woody Tircuit, Ron Trees, Carl Wicker, Al Wickman, John Wilcox, Dale Wrisley, Jim Yeomans.

John Warden and associates in Greece en route to Saudi Arabia (Left to right): John Warden, Ben Harvey, Dave Deptula, Ronnie Stanfill

After leaving the Air Force in 1995, I started a company called Venturist, Inc., to deliver what later became the Prometheus Process. My daughter Betsy left Fidelity Investments in New York to help me start and run the business; her contributions as Executive Vice President have been extraordinary. Mike Cline, who had been with me at the Air Command and Staff College, joined the new company as our Chief Software Architect; his work in developing Prometheus software has been more than impressive. Richard Reynolds, author of *Heart of the Storm,* worked with us for over a year before starting his own company; he helped refine and polish the ideas. Howard Guiles, who had been with me at the Air Command and Staff College and was also a fellow student at National War College, joined us three years ago as our Chief Financial Officer.

Since 1996, when I first started working with companies to help them think strategically, a number of the people in our client companies have made special contributions to developing and clarifying the strategy process. Flint Dille introduced me to Electronic Arts, where he and his associates used the Five Rings idea to help them construct a hugely successful computer game, Soviet Strike. Flint and I also worked together to build another game called Hyper-War—which in turn led to more precision and clarity in my strategic thinking. Ray Gumpert, then head of training and organizational effectiveness for Texas Instruments' Semiconductor Group, brought Perry Smith—author, former CNN commentator, former Commandant of the National War College, personal friend and mentor, and first true promoter of the air campaign—and me to TI and guided us through the first year of our work with that company. George Consolver, Texas Instruments' Director of strategy process, worked with us extensively and provided many great suggestions. Mary Davis, former Vice Chairman of Jannotte, Bray & Associates and later head of her own high-end executive consulting and coaching company, Davis Consulting Group LLC, helped me with my business start-ups and with the Prometheus concepts. I joined her to assist one of her clients, Prudential Bank, to develop its strategy. She then introduced me to Larry Small, then President of FannieMae and later Secretary of the Smithsonian Institution. Larry spent two days with the process and made many helpful suggestions. It was just after our work with FannieMae that we named our process Prometheus to capture the importance and excitement of strategic thinking and execution.

Leland Russell and I began working together in 1998. Sandy Tennant, CEO of Nefilim Associates, introduced us to Jay Cashman and provided great marketing ideas. Jay Cashman used Prometheus twice, once for his large construction company and the second time for his Internet start-up, Dirtpile.com. Gary Esolen and Valerie LeBlanc, on Sandy's recommendation, used Prometheus to do the up-front strategic planning for their Internet start-up, TravelPlace.com, and again provided many helpful ideas. Our first clients as Prometheus Strategies, Inc., were EPS and McDonald's. At the former, Walter Schindler provided many great ideas, which have continued since he founded Odyssey Strategic Partners, an innovative venture capital company. Wayne Wolf, then head of McDonald's U.S. supply chain group, brought us to McDonald's, where Ted Nagengast excelled in helping us make Prometheus work for a big, diverse company. Ted's help and advice were of the highest caliber and value. Thereafter, Monica Boyles, Vice President for franchisee relationships, became the Prometheus Orchestrator for Mike Roberts's west division of McDonald's. Her ideas, enthusiasm, and support have been priceless.

While with McDonald's, we also had the opportunity to work with The Bama Companies, McDonald's supplier of pastry desserts and biscuits. The Bama CEO and co-owner, Paula Marshall-Chapman, was one of the most effective and eager change agents we have met. She spearheaded her company's move into *FastTime* Prometheus with exceptional verve and élan and gave us many additional ideas of what could be done when the CEO is truly involved. Also at Bama, Denny Donahue served as the company's very capable campaign orchestrator and again showed us how much could be accomplished by someone who is motivated and smart.

At Bama, I had the pleasure for the first time of working with Leland's sister, Debra Russell. At Bama and in other venues, Debra helped our client groups grasp and embrace the Prometheus process. Horst Abraham, a former Olympic ski coach and a world-class consultant in his own right, who attended several of our sessions, invariably asked incisive questions, which led to more and more precision in our thinking.

All the foregoing gets us to this book. Our most sincere thanks to Vivien Ravdin, former Senior Editor at *Reader's Digest,* for all her help and suggestions. John and Ellen Piazza, both of whom had made many contributions to national security when John was on the Air Staff and Ellen was the Secretary of the Air Force's speech-writer, helped us assemble the first drafts of the book and gave us many substantive ideas to improve it. Debby Flora of Venturist,

Inc., developed the graphic for the jacket. Of course, we would not be at this point without the yeoman effort of our editor *extraordinaire* Bill Simon (a best-selling author in his own right), who brought together the frequently disorganized efforts of Leland and me. At this point, Venturist's Executive VP, my daughter Betsy, recognized that we would not make our deadlines without someone assuming the role of director, coordinator, super-editor, mediator, and motivator. She assumed all of these duties while supervising the introduction of a new software program. Without her efforts this book would have been delayed for many months. Our newest associate, Pat Mauney, a former McDonald's owner/operator, also made many substantive contributions.

For the coauthor of *Winning in FastTime*, Leland Russell, I reserve the last thanks. I had for some time planned to write a book about the Prometheus Process but could never carve out sufficient time to assemble and integrate transcripts of my lectures, various short pieces, and hundreds of presentation slides to make it happen. In late 1999, after Leland and I had formed Prometheus Strategies, Inc., we decided that Leland would concentrate on the book project while I concentrated on the fieldwork. Twelve months later the book was a reality—which would not have happened without Leland's dedication and hard work. Leland—thanks!

—*John Warden*

Acknowledgments

Working on *Winning in FastTime* has been an exciting and reward-ing journey. What I remember most are the many extraordinary people I've encountered along the way. First and foremost, I would like to thank my business partner and coauthor, John Warden, from whom I've learned so much, for entrusting me to build upon the concepts he originally developed. John's daughter Betsy (for whom all is possible) was instrumental in our relationship from the begin-ning, and in the final days of the writing of the manuscript her graceful power helped us "bring it home."

Winning in FastTime was a monumental team effort. How lucky we were to have the detailed advice and creative contributions of so many gifted and enthusiastic people during the year it took for the manuscript to come to fruition. We are truly grateful for their efforts.

Best-selling author and Global Business Book Award nominee William Simon may rival Job for star billing in the area of patience and forgiveness. John and I heaped so many changes into Bill's e-mail inbox at the very last minute that it's a miracle he had the enduring strength to put up with it all. Bill's insight, judgment, and a calmly assured work style made an enormous difference in the ultimate quality and readability of our manuscript.

Throughout the writing of the book we turned to Vivien Ravdin, a skilled writer and editor in the fields of business and national policy and a former senior editor at *Reader's Digest*. Vivien also brought a unique, bird's-eye view of the dramatic events at the heart of our book: She was speechwriter, then chief speechwriter, to the Secretary of Defense during Desert Storm and its aftermath. Her deep understanding of John's pioneering strategic ideas as well as of my model for change management helped us join two dynamic streams of thought into the power that is Prometheus.

Our heartfelt thanks also goes to two people whose enthusiasm and creative contributions rose to the level of inspiration. The insights and expertise of retired Air Force Colonel John Piazza and his wife, Ellen, illuminated many of the ideas in the book. John Piazza worked for John Warden during the genesis of the Prometheus concepts and now applies them with extraordinary success for a nonprofit organization. Ellen is a writer whose elegant economy of words contrasts with an unlimited willingness to explore and discuss ideas. She sparked discovery and backlit the early manuscript with her research, interviews, and scholarship.

We would also like to acknowledge our graphics team for their exceptional contributions. Debby Flora of Venturist, Inc., developed the illustrations for the book. Rita Swanson helped us refine the jacket and designed the part title pages. Harushi Matsui of Spiderweb Digital Studio in collaboration with Frank Carson designed two of the graphics for the Prometheus Imperatives. Also Frank Carson deserves special acknowledgment for suggesting the idea of articulating the Promethic laws.

My personal path to *Winning in FastTime* began in 1990 when the concept of "creating the future" first became a fire in my mind. I am forever indebted to my longtime partner, Gordon Walker, and my friend William Shatner of *Star Trek* fame for their unwavering support in producing the national leadership forum *A Day in the Future* and the video program *Tearing Down the Walls*. Those projects not only galvanized my thinking on the new realities and the new patterns of thinking we need to be successful, they also launched my career in change management and strategy deployment.

Through the past ten years of research, writing, and producing programs on change, a number of people helped me build the base of knowledge I called upon in the writing of this book. Jim Bolt, Chairman of Executive Development Associates, was my mentor in the early years and introduced me to many of the thought leaders in the field of executive education and to many of my clients, including BellSouth, Sun Microsystems, Hewlett-Packard, and Texas Instruments. I am deeply indebted to two Texas Instruments executives, George Consolver, Director of Strategy, and John Baum, Director of Executive Education, who introduced me to John Warden in 1997, suggesting that our talents might be complementary. I am also grateful to John Byers of Texas Instruments' Office of Best Practices for providing an endless stream of "knowledge bytes" on leadership and strategic thinking.

My friend Kathryn Johnson, CEO of the Health Forum, has been an inspiration and a supporter for more than a decade. Kathryn has continually fired off my neurons by exposing me to new cutting-edge leadership concepts and to many of the leading lights in the health-care field and beyond. Two of those people, Dr. Don Berwick and Maureen Bisognano, coleaders of Institute for Healthcare Improvement, also deserve special thanks for their support and the knowledge they have shared. Although we met only briefly, I would also like to thank Peter Senge for introducing me to the discipline of system thinking. It was this knowledge that allowed me to recognize instantly the power and importance of John Warden's Five Rings model.

I am deeply indebted to many other successful leaders and cutting-edge thinkers from whom I've learned so much over the past decade. One of the standouts is Doug Engelbart, who was the first to envision, in the 1950s, people sitting in front of displays, "flying around" in an information space where they could formulate and organize their ideas with incredible speed and flexibility. Doug helped me understand the past and future of information technology. Having a personal dialogue with one of the great technology visionaries of our time—the father of the word processor, the mouse, and graphical computing and an inventor of the Internet—was an extraordinary learning experience.

The late Ned Herrmann, manager of management education for GE and a pioneer of creative thinking in the corporation, first opened my eyes to the burgeoning research in human development and its importance in mastering change. Ned's cornucopia of knowledge about thinking and learning styles, brain function, and individual and group creativity, as well as his great compassion, left an indelible impression and has affected all of my work.

Since 1997 my gifted friend and colleague Horst Abraham has unselfishly shared his considerable knowledge in the areas of personal mastery, mental models, and action learning (which he calls "learning from the neck down"). Horst helped us shape the Prometheus consulting model and, over the past year, the manuscript for this book.

The practical experience that allowed us to focus the lessons of Desert Storm for the battlefield of twenty-first-century business came from the opportunities over the years to learn from our clients— there are more than we could ever list. Especially helpful for this project was Brian Baker, former head of Mobil's North American operations, who shared his experience with using strategic performance measures to drive a massive corporate turnaround, and the many members of McDonald's corporate staff, suppliers and franchisees who applied the Prometheus concepts and gave us ongoing feedback as we developed the manuscript.

When John and I launched our consulting partnership, John Mroz, President of the Institute for East West Studies, was our very first client. The weekend we spent with his board of directors at John Kluge's Virginia estate, Morven, in April of 1998 was an auspicious beginning and a confirmation of the power of the Prometheus concepts. We are also indebted to another early client, Andy Riddell, CEO of Atlanticare Medical Center, for his willingness to try a radical idea—applying the planning process used in Desert Storm to the challenges in health care.

During the course of writing, several people agreed to extensive interviews, and their wisdom and insights are reflected in the finished book. Sandy Ogg, Corporate Vice President and Director of Motorola's Office of Leadership, was very generous with his time and gave us some excellent ideas. General Dave Deptula, one of the brilliant Air Force officers who was not only an integral part of the original Checkmate planning team in Washington, but also at the heart of the planning and execution effort in Riyadh, was very generous with his time and helped us illuminate the concept of Desired Effects. Jason Amoriell, the intelligence expert who instructed agencies like the Kansas City Drug Enforcement Agency, the New York Police Department, and the Montgomery, Alabama, task force in the use of the Five Rings, showed how the Five Rings model could be universally applied. Game designer and author Flint Dille not only shared his personal experience in applying the Prometheus concepts, he also contributed some terrific ideas that helped us shape the introduction of the book.

I am especially grateful to my colleagues from the Learning Network who reviewed the manuscript and offered excellent advice on how to improve it. Dr. Quinn Mills of Harvard University and Dr. Robert Fulmer of Pepperdine University both suggested that we keep the focus on the Prometheus Process and include more business examples. We heeded their advice and it made all the difference. Early on, Sally Helgesen, a dear friend and best-selling author (of *The Female Advantage* and *The Web of Inclusion*), reviewed the work to date and made several structural suggestions that affected the overall direction of the manuscript. Over the past year, Ron Meeks of Executive Development Associates provided a fresh perspective whenever one was needed. My heartfelt thanks for advice on the manuscript also goes to Marcy Callaway, Chris Cappy, Rick Culley, Alyssa Freas, Lenny Lind, Willie Olivieri, Candace Palmer-lee, Tara Rethore, Lisa Robbins, and Roosevelt Thomas.

It seems highly appropriate to end these acknowledgments by thanking the people who helped me personally navigate the nineties and arrive at a point where I could make a creative contribution to *Winning in FastTime*. My deepest thanks goes to my long-time friend Elizabeth Weber and my cousin Tom Sutton, who have been stalwart supporters on a personal and a business level for many years. My multitalented sister, Debra Russell, has contributed so much to Prometheus and to my life that I can never thank her sufficiently. Last, I would like to acknowledge the two miracles in my life: my wife, Melissa, and my son, Simon. Their patience, honesty, sense of humor, and forgiveness has made this journey possible.

—*Leland A. Russell*

A

Abraham, Horst, 211, 216
Across-the-board impact, 113
Action, Time Value of, 41–43
Action learning, 194
Action plan for Center of Gravity, 132–133
Agents in Five Rings model, 112, 114, 115, 120–121, 135
Air travel industry
  frequent-flyer programs in, 25
  Parallel Approach in, 44–45
  Prime Directives in, 82
  strategic evaluation of events in, 98–99
  strategies in, 24–26, 26
  tactical competition in, 24–25
Aleinikov, Andrei, 71
Alexander, Minter, 206
Alexander the Great, 36
Allen, Charles, 205
Altshuller, Genrich, 70
Amazon.com, 58, 64
Amoriell, Jason, 114, 217
Apple computers, competition between IBM-compatible PCs and, 27
Architectural thinking, 6, 65–66, 179–182
Assumptions, addressing, in the environment, 59–61
Atlanticare Medical Center, 216
Automobile industry
  Japanese in, 26–27
  strategies in, 26–27
Axiomatic Behavior, 87–88

B

Baker, Brian, 95, 216
Baldridge, Malcolm, National Quality Award, 29
Balkans, staying out of, 185–186
Bama Companies, 83–85, 195, 211
Barnes & Noble, 23
Baum, John, 34, 215
Behavioral expectations, articulating, 16, 78, 79
BellSouth, 215
Benchmarking, global, 58–59

Berwick, Don, 215
Bezos, Jeff, 64
Bisognano, Maureen, 215
Boeing Corporation, 44
Boiler-Frog Syndrome, 27
Bottom-up thinking, 179
Boyles, Monica, 211
Brands, 67, 69, 105
Braniff, 98
Brick-and-mortar retailers, 23
Budget process, Open Planning approach in, 193–194
Bureaucracy, Parallel Campaigns as antidote to, 142
Burger King, 44
Bush, George, 11, 21, 205
Business, Axiomatic Behaviors in, 87–88
  brands in, 67, 69, 105
  business areas of, 66–67, 68, 103
  Calculated Rules in, 87
  characteristics of systems in, 33–34
  corporate citizenship in, 67, 69, 105
  corporate culture in, 67, 69, 105
  direction of change in, 51–53
  disruption of equilibrium in, 35–36
  disruptive innovations in, 55–57
  effects-based planning in, 127–128, 130–131
  financial position of, 66, 68, 103
  Future Picture for, 63
  Guiding Precepts for, 77–89
  incentive philosophy in, 67, 69, 106
  innovation in, 67, 68–69, 79, 104
  key to success in, 29
  leverage points in, 17, 36–39
  looking for new ways of doing, 195
  market position, 66, 68, 103
  measuring success in, 16–17
  need for changes in gameplan, 20–31
  new way of running, 5–7
  outsider perception for, 67, 69, 104
  ownership of, 67, 69, 105
  Parallel Approach in, 44–45
  Prime Directives in, 81–83
  revolutionary precision in, 57–59

Rules of Engagement in, 83–85
stakeholder perception in, 67, 69, 104
systems perspective for, 17
taking the offensive in, 181–182
time-compression and, 53–55
workforce characteristics for, 67, 69, 104
Business cycles, compression of, 55
Business model, making changes in, 22
Business organization
    Agents ring in, 120
    Five Rings map of typical, 122–123
    Infrastructure ring in, 118
    Leadership ring of, 116–117
    Population ring in, 119, 135
    Processes ring in, 117, 134–135
Byers, John, 215

C
Calculated Rules, 87
Campaign. See also Parallel campaigns
    defined, 141
    executing plans for, 152
    mind-set for, 147
    multiple, 141
    for winning, 192
Campaign plan, executing, 152
Campaign rooms, 145–146
    virtual, 146
Campaign teams, commissioning, 143
Campaign to Win imperative, 47
    organizing for success in, 152–163
    parallel campaigns in, 141–151
Cannae, Battle of, 90–91
Cardinal rules, 179–190
    architectural thinking, 6, 65–66, 179–182
    executing "good enough" plans, 180–181
    exploiting key force, 186–187
    imposing plan, 182–185
    indirect approach, 184–185
    maintaining and using reserves, 187–190
    in maintaining momentum, 189–190

staying out of the Balkans, 185–186
    taking the offensive, 181–182
Career success, key to, 29
Cashman, Jay, 210
CATIA (computer-aided three-dimensional interactive application), 44
Centers of Gravity. See Leverage points
Change
    cost of, 160–161
    direction of, in environment, 51–53
    high-velocity, 161–162
    leverage points in, 36–39
    making, in gameplan, 20–31
    parallel approach to, 39–41
    resisting, 156
    serial approach to, 39, 43, 142, 162
    speed and complexity of, 64
Charles Schwab, 20, 37
Cheney, Richard, 205
Chivas, 99
Christensen, Clayton, 56, 153–154
Clausewitz, Carl von, 36–37
Click-and-mortar retailers, 23, 37
Closed-door planning versus open-door planning, 73–75
Commitment, demonstrating, 195–196
Communication, role of Red Team in, 148–149
Compaq, 22, 27
Competency, 194
Competition
    discerning strategic moves by, 26
    tactical, 24–25
Competitive advantage, 25, 54
Computer industry, time compression in, 53–54
Computer memory-chip business, 25
    Moor's Law and, 52
Concurrent engineering, 44
Consolver, George, 210, 215
Corporate citizenship, 67, 69, 105
Corporate culture, 67, 69, 105
Course, staying the, in the Future Picture, 75
Crown Royal, 99

D

Davis, Mary, 210
Davis Consulting Group, 210
Death by delay phenomenon, 43
Decision making
  empowered, 6
  on Future Picture, 15
  Guiding Precepts in, 80–81
  Open Planning and, 15
Declaration of Independence, 80
Declining returns, 174
Defense, U.S. Department of, 101
Dell, Michael, 99–100
Dell Computers, 20, 22, 26, 27,
  99–100, 156
Deptula, Dave, 128, 130, 158,
  206–207, 216
Desert Storm
  air campaign in, ix, 9, 32–33
  application of strategic planning
    in, 9–19
  assault on Centers of Gravity in, 41
  encircling maneuver used by, 90–91
  Five Rings analysis in, 134–135
  large-scale integrated planning for,
    13
  measuring success in, 16–17
  parallel approach in, 17–18
  Prime Directives in, 82
  recognizing end in, 18
  revolutionary precision and, 57
  rules of engagement in, 85–86
Design the Future imperative, 15, 47
  environment in, 51–62
  Future Picture in, 63–76
  Guiding Precepts in, 77–89
  Measures of Merit in, 90–106
Desired Effects, 127–137
  Campaign Mind-Set in, 147
  defined, 131–132
  determining, 131–132
  leveraging available resources,
    128–130
  power of precision targeting and,
    133–139
  prioritizing Centers of Gravity,
    135–136
  system "energy events," 130–131
Destination. See Future Picture

Digital signal processors (DSPs), 30
Dille, Flint, 114, 115, 210
Direct approach, 184
Direction of change in the environ-
  ment, 51–53
Directions, developing high-level, 132
Dirtpile.com, 210
Disney, Walt, Company, 173
Disruptive innovations in the envi-
  ronment, 55–57
Donahue, Denny, 195, 211
dot.com retailers, strategy of, 23
DreamWorks SKG, 38–39, 155
Dugan, Michael C., 206
Dynamic systems, resistance of
  change by, 35

E

eBay, 26
e-commerce
  precision revolution in, 57–58
  web-based auctions in, 58
Economic environment, 60
Effects-based planning, 127–128,
  129–130
Effects-based targeting, 131–132
Elastic limit, breaking, 195
Electronic Arts, 114, 210
Empowered decision making, 6
Endgame, 167–178
  declining returns for, 174
  defining exit points for, 170–171
  exiting on top with style, 177–178
  market shifts for, 175–177
  planning for, 167, 168
  valuation zenith for, 171–173
Endpoints, recognizing, in strategic
  planning, 18–19
Ends, measurement of, 93–94
Enemies, choosing, 183–184
Engelbart, Doug, 215
Engibous, Tom, 29–30
Entrepreneurs, 85
Environment, 51–62
  addressing assumptions n, 59–61
  direction of change in, 51–53
  disruptive innovations in, 55–57
  economic, 60
  political, 60

revolutionary precision in, 57–59
scoping the, 51, 61, 63
technological, 61
time-compression in, 53–55
Epimetheus (Greek god), 3
EPS, 211
Esolen, Gary, 210
Events, strategic evaluation of, 98–99
Executive Development Associates, 217
Exit points
    declining returns as, 174
    defining, 170–171, 193
    market shifts as, 175–177
    valuation zenith as, 171–173
External measures, using, 100–102
ExxonMobil, 95

F
FannieMae, 210
Fast food industry, tactical moves in, 25
Financial position, 66, 68, 103
Financial returns, declining, as exit point, 174
Finish with Finesse imperative, 47, 193
    cardinal rules in, 179–190
    endgame in, 167–178
Finite life span for Future Pictures, 64
First-mover advantage, 181
Five Rings model, 109–126, 111–113
    agents in, 112, 114, 115, 120–121, 135
    infrastructure in, 112, 114, 115, 118, 135
    leadership in, 112, 114, 115, 116–117, 134
    methods of using, 121–124
    population in, 112, 114, 115, 119–120
    power of precision targeting and, 133–139
    in practice, 116–121
    processes in, 112, 114, 115, 117–118, 134–135
    system-mapping process and, 124–126
    targeting Centers of Gravity, 109,

110–111
    as universal tool, 114–116
Flexibility
    in leadership, 84
    strategic, 154–155
Flora, Debby, 211
Ford Motor, 169
Fox, Roger B., 205
Frequent-flyer programs, 25
Friends, choosing, 183–184
From/to charts, 110
Fulmer, Robert, 217
Future Picture, 63–76, 91
    architectural thinking in, 65–66
    componenents of, 66–68
    decision making on, 15
    designing your, 191–192
    developing Measures of Merit for components of, 102–106
    disruptive innovations in, 55–57
    finite life span for, 64
    focusing on, 188–189
    ideal final result for, 70–71
    making decisions in view of, 77
    Open Planning for, 71–73
    revolutionary precision in, 57–59
    staying the course in, 75
    synthesis of into statement for, 68–70
    time-compression and, 53–55

G
Game-changing organizations
    advantages of, 20
    advantages of strategy for, 25–27
    characteristics of, 20–21
    leadership in, 28–31
    sine qua non of winning, 28
    strategy of, 21–22, 28–31
    tactics versus strategy for, 22–23
    38th-parallel phenomenon in, 23–25
Game-changing strategy, 11, 19, 23–25
Gameplan, making changes in, 20–31
Gates, Bill, 37, 56, 154
Gateway, 27
General Electric, 59, 83, 215–216
General Motors, 154, 170
Geopolitics, exit strategy and, 173

Gilmore, Merle, 158–159
Global benchmarking, 58–59
Grand Strategy, 5, 6
ground rules for, 82
  as key to sustainable competitive
    advantage, 28
  painting the Future Picture as step
    in planning, 64
Groupthink, 148–149
Grove, Andy, 56
Guiding Precepts, 15–16, 77–89
  conditions for, 80
  defined, 79
  engraving, 75, 79–81, 86–88
  Prime Directives in, 81–83
  Rules of Engagement for, 83–85
Gulf War. See Desert Storm
Gumpert, Ray, 210

H
Haas, Richard, 205
Hammel, Gary, 28–29
Hannibal, 90–91, 91, 92, 98
Hartmann, Frederick H., 205
Harvey, Ben, 207
Hayden, Michael, 206
Health Forum, 215
Helgesen, Sally, 217
Herbold, Bob, 79
Hermann, Ned, 215–216
Hewlett-Packard, 27, 153–154, 215
High-velocity change, 161–162
Hippocrates, 81
Horner, Charles, 206, 207
Horner, Chuck, 13
Human body
  Agents ring in, 120
  Infrastructure ring in, 118
  Leadership ring in, 116
  Population ring in, 119
  Processes ring in, 117
Hussein, Saddam, 10, 13, 14, 21, 40,
  158
Hyper-Change, ix, 52–53
Hysteresis Effect, 35

I
IBM, 26, 154
IBM-compatible PCs, 26, 87

competition between Apple com
  puters and, 27
strategic basis for, 27
Ideal final result, 70–71
Incentive philosophy, 67, 69, 106
Indirect approach, 26–27, 184–185
Inertia, law of, 45
Information
  gathering meaningful, reliable, 132
  guidelines for accelerating flow of,
    160
  intelligent attitude toward, 157
  need for accurate, in serial
    approach, 43
  organizing to exploit, 157–160
  serial flow of essential, 159–160
Information technology, exposition
  in, 52–53
Infrastructure in Five Rings model,
  112, 114, 115, 118, 135
Innovation, 67, 68–69, 104
  delivering, 79
Instant Thunder, 9–19
  challenge in, 9–12
  designing the future approach, 15
  focus on Centers of Gravity in, 17
  guiding principles in, 15–16
  measuring success in, 16–17
  open planning approach in, 14–15
  origin of term, 9
  parallel approach in, 17–18
  planning for victory, 12–14
  recognizing endpoints in, 18–19
  systems perspective in, 17
Institute for East West Studies, 216
Intel, 29, 30, 56, 79–80, 173
Intelligence, defined, 157
Internal-change approach, 33
Iridium, 43

J
Jamaica Hospital Medical Center, 184
Japanese, in automobile industry,
  26–27
Java, 154
Jefferson, Thomas, 80
Johnson, Karhtyn, 215

K
Katzenberg, Jeffrey, 155
Kelleher, Herb, 26
Kissel, Chuck, 207
Kluge, John, 216
Kroc, Ray, 113

L
Language, learning, 196–197
Large-scale integrated planning, 13
Leader(s)
    Campaign Orchestrator as,
        144–145, 147
    role of, in system targeting, 111
Leader-defined initiatives, 110
Leadership
    in Five Rings model, 112, 114, 115,
        116–117, 134
    need for flexibility in, 84
    role of, in pushing organization
        past elastic limit, 195
    strategy and, 28–31
LeBlanc, Valerie, 210
Leverage points, 14, 17, 21, 32–47
    action plan for, 132–133
    in business, 22
    Campaign Mind-Set in, 147
    effects-based planning and,
        127–128
    effects on, 36–39
    energy events for, 130–131
    focusing on, 17
    multiple, 37, 110, 128
    parallel approach to, 39–41, 128
    prioritizing, 135–136
    Promethic Laws and, 109–110
    in Rive Rings model, 113
    strategic sucess and, 92
    targeting, 109, 110–111
Leveraging of available resources,
    128–130
Loh, John Mike, 12, 13, 206
Long-term thinking, 77
Luttwak, Edward N., 205

M
MacArthur, Douglas, 23–24
Macro-trends, 52
Maharbal, 91

Mano a mano solution, 21
Manufacturing-and-services industry,
    sigma performance levels in, 58–59
Marino, Dan, 169
Market
    Agents ring in, 120
    Five Rings map of typical, 124, 125
    Infrastructure ring in, 118
    Leadership ring in, 117
    Population ring in, 119
    Processes ring in, 118
    testing waters in, 183
Market capitalization, 30
Marketplace dynamics, 60
    Rules of Engagement and, 86
Market position, 66, 68, 103
Market shifts, 175–177
Marshall-Chapman, Paula, 113, 211
McDonald's, 25, 83–85, 113, 115, 146,
    193, 211, 212, 216
MCI WorldCom, 20
McPeak, Tony, 206
Measures of Merit. See Strategic meas-
    urements
Meeks, Ron, 217
Melville, John, 156
Merrill Lynch, 37–38
Microsoft, 20, 26, 79, 154–155,
    183–184
Military plans, development of, 10, 12
Military rules of engagement, 85–86
Mills, Quinn, 217
Mind-set
    campaign, 147
    strategic, 7, 96, 147
    system, 109
    tactical, 97
Mission creep, 18
Mobil Oil, 95, 216
Momentum
    maintaining, 189–190
    precision revolution in building, 59
Moore's Law, 52
Mother Teresa, 77
Motorola, 29, 43, 58–59, 84, 158, 216
    parallel campaigns at, 142–143
Mroz, John, 216
Multiplicity, in Parallel Campaigns, 40,
    142

N

Nagengast, Ted, 193, 211
Nation-state
    Agents ring in, 120
    Infracture ring in, 118
    Leadership ring of, 116
    Population ring in, 119
    Processes ring in, 117
Nefilim Associates, 210
Negative-energy event, 130
Netscape, 155
New product development, 63, 70–71
Nintendo, 44
Numbers, power of, 71–72

O

Obstacles, bypassing, 189–190
Odyssey Strategic Partners, 211
Offensive action
    need for quick, 11
    taking, 181–182
Ogg, Sandy, 84, 143, 158, 216
Open Planning, 12, 14–15, 71–73, 88, 135
    in budget process, 193–194
    closed-door planning versus, 73–75
    cost of change and, 160
    decision making and, 15
    guidelines for, 72–73
Organizational change, parallel operations in, 161–162
Organizational structure, 152–163
    cost of change and, 160–161
    creating new, 155–156
    high-velocity change and, 161–162
    information exploitation and, 157–160
    in new situations, 153–154
    new technologies in, 155–156
    resisting change in, 156
    strategic flexibility in, 154–155
    value of, 153–154
Organization audits, 110
Outsider perception, 67, 69, 104
Ownership, 67, 69, 105

P

Parallel Campaigns, 128, 136, 141–151
    as antidote to resource limitations, 41–44

in business, 44–45
campaign mind-set for, 147
campaign room for, 145–146
in effecting Centers of Gravity, 39–41
at Motorola, 142–143
multiplicity in, 40, 142
Orchestrator for, 144–145, 147
Red Team for, 148–149
in review, 149–150
simultaneity in, 40, 142
in strategic planning, 17–18
Three-Echelon Rule for, 147–148
Participation, cost of, 182–183
Perry, Bill, 173
Piazza, Ellen, 211
Piazza, John, 211
Plan(s)
    executing campaign, 152
    executing "good enough," 180–181
    imposing your, 182–185
Planning. See also Strategic planning
    closed-door versus open-door, 73–75
    effects based, 127–128, 130–131
    Five Rings approach to systems, 115–116
    large-scale integrated, 13
    open, 12, 14–15, 71–75, 88, 135, 160
    termination, 19
Political environment, 60
Population, in Five Rings model, 112, 114, 115, 119–120, 135
Positive-energy event, 130
Powell, Colin, 13, 206
Prahalad, C. K., 28–29
Precision targeting, power of, 133–139
Prime Directives in Guiding Precepts, 81–83
Proactive approach, 181–182
Processes in Five Rings model, 112, 114, 115, 117–118
Product diffusion, 54–55
Product fixation, 176
Product-marketing approach, 33
Product obsession, 56
Progress, strategic measurement of, 16–17
Project team, creation of Future Picture for, 63, 70–71

Prometheus (Greek god), 3–4
Prometheus Process, 3–8
  applying, 193–194
  basis for assumptions in, 5
  benefits of, 6
  birth of, ix
  Campaign to Win imperative in,
    47, 141–163
  defined, ix, 5, 8
  Design the Future imperative in,
    47, 51–106
  Finish with Finesse imperative in,
    47, 167–190
  future picture in, 63–76
  selection of name, 3–4
  Target for Success imperative in,
    47, 167–190
Promethic Laws, 45–46, 109–110, 167
Prudential Bank, 210
Pushing the envelope, 64

Q
Quality, Six Sigma program and,
  58–59

R
Reactive approach, 182
Reagan, Ronald, 75
Red team, 148–149
Reserves, maintaining and using,
  187–190
Resources
  estimating requirements, 132
  leveraging available, 128–130
  parallel approach as antidote to
    limitations, 41–44
  targeting against Centers of
    Gravity, 17
Revolutionary precision in the envi-
  ronment, 57–59
Rice, Donald, 205
Rissell, Andy, 216
Roberts, Mike, 211
Rolling Thunder, 12
Rules of Engagement, 83–85
  military, 85–86
Russell, Debra, 211
Russell, Leland, 210, 212
Ruth, Babe, 168

S
Samsung, 30
Schindler, Walter, 211
Schwarzkopf, Norman, 9–10, 11,
  12–13, 21, 71–72, 145, 186–187, 206
Scoping the environment, 51, 61, 63
Sea changes, 61
Seinfield, Jerry, 168–169
Seismic shift
  disruptive innovation as, 55–57
  revolutionary precision as, 57–59
  time-compression as, 53–55
Sell over the Net tactic, 23
Senge, Peter, 34
Serbia, serial war against, 42
Serial approach to change, 39, 43,
  142, 162
Serial flow of essential information,
  159–160
Simultaneity in Parallel Campaigns,
  40, 142
Sine qua non of winning, 28
Single-point failures, 40
Sisyphus syndrome, 34–36
Six Sigma program, 58–59
Sloan, Alfred, 170
Small, Larry, 210
Smirnoff, 99
Smith, Perry M., 207, 210
Smithsonian Institution, 210
Southwest Airlines, 26, 98–99
Sparta, 81
Stakeholder perception, 67, 69, 104
Stanfill, Ronnie, 207
Strategic evaluation of events, 98–99
Strategic flexibility, 154–155
Strategic integration, role of leader in,
  144
Strategic linkage, 131
Strategic measurements, 16–17, 90–106
  building, 99–100
  clarifying, 132
  developing, 102–106
  ends not means in, 93–94, 129
  establishing, 92–93
  evaluating events in, 98–99
  external measures as, 100–102
  purpose of, 93
  resisting change and, 156
  strategic perspective of, 96–97

for strategic success, 16–17, 91–92
   tactical measures as, 94–96
Strategic mind-set, 7, 96, 147
Strategic moves, difficulty in discerning, 26
Strategic objectives, defining, 15
Strategic perspective, 96–97
Strategic planning, 5, 9–19. See also
   Planning
   application of, in Desert Storm, 9–19
   challenge in, 9–12
   designing the future approach to, 15
   focus on Centers of Gravity in, 17
   Future Picture in, 63–64
   guiding principles for, 15–16
   Open Planning approach in, 14–15
   origin of term, 9
   parallel approach in, 17–18
   planning for victory, 12–14
   Prime Directives in, 82
   recognizing endpoints in, 18–19
   systems perspective in, 17
Strategic success, measuring, 16–17,
   91–92
Strategic targets, selecting right, 111
Strategic thinking
   addressing assumptions in, 59–61
   need for common framework for, 6
Strategy
   advantages of, 25–27
   creating winning system, 33–34
   game-changing, 23–25
   interrelated elements in, 26
   leadership and, 28–31
   mistaking tactics for, 23–25
   as superior approach, 21–22
   tactics versus, 22–23
Success. See also Organizational structure
   measuring strategic, 16–17, 91–92
   Parallel Campaigns in concentrating for, 142
   tactical, 92, 93, 127
   targeting for, 192
   Time Value of Action and, 41–43
Sun Microsystems, 154, 215
Sustainable competitive advantage,
   28–31
System(s)
   characteristics of, 33–34

creating winning strategies, 33
disruption of equilibrium in, 35–36
elastic limits of, 35
"energy events" in, 130–131
resilience of, 35
System change, 34
System-mapping process, 124–126
System mind-set, 109
System perspective, 17
Systems planning, Five Rings
   approach to, 115–116
System strategy, Five Rings model in
   developing, 114–116
System targeting, leader's role in, 111
System thinking
   defined, 34
   Five Rings model and, 112

T
Tactical competition, 24–25
   recognition of, 25
Tactical environment, survival in, 23
Tactical excellence, importance of,
   22–23
Tactical measures, 93, 94–96
Tactical mind-set, 97
Tactical success, 92, 93, 99, 127
Tactics
   agents and, 120–121
   defined, 22
   mistaking, for strategy, 23–25
   as responsibility of campaign planner, 132
   versus strategy, 22–23
Target for Success imperative, 47
   desired effects, 127–137
   five rings in, 109–126
Taylor, Dan, 207
Technological environment, 61
Technology
   exit strategy and, 171–173
   resistance to new, 156
Templeton, Rich, 29–30
Ten Commandments, 82
Tennant, Sandy, 210
Termination planning, lack of, 19
Termination points, 142
Texas Instruments, 34, 115, 210, 215
   strategic moves at, 29–31
Thinking. See also Strategic thinking

architectural, 6, 65–66, 179–182
bottom-up, 180
like a winner, 197
top-down, 179–180
38th-parallel phenomenon, 23–25
3M Corporation, 82
Three-echelon rule, 147–148, 159
Time compression, 53–55
Time frame, deciding on, 132
Time is money phenomenon, 43
Time Value of Action, 41–43, 55, 161
Timing, importance of, 188
Top-down thinking, 179–180
TravelPlace.com, 210–211
Trim-tab effect, 133–139
TWA, 24

V
Value, finding point of maximum,
    171–173
Venturist, 211
Vietnam War
    determining victory in, 28
    measuring success in, 16, 92
    Rolling Thunder plan in, 12
Virtual campaign rooms, 146

W
Walk the talk, 88
Wang Laboratories, 65
Warden, John, 10–11, 13, 15, 71–72,
    97, 111, 115, 129, 144–145, 146,
    158
Web-based auctions, 58
Welch, Jack, 59
Wendy's, 25
Winner, thinking like, 197
Winning, 179
    campaign for, 192
    planning for, 12–13
    sine qua non of, 28
Workforce characteristics, 67, 69, 104
World War I, 169–170
    serial action in, 42
World War II
    measuring ends in, 93–94
    precision in, 57

Y
Yahoo!, 26, 155

HOW TO CONTACT THE AUTHORS

John Warden and Leland Russell each provide consulting services through their own independent consulting companies. Please send all requests for information about these services, as well as inquiries about their availability for speeches and seminars, to them at the addresses below. Comments and ideas are welcome.

John Warden
8233 Old Federal Road
Montgomery, AL 36117
Tel: (334)272-9800
Fax: (334)277-6400
www.venturist.com
jwarden@venturist.com

Leland Russell
4750 Von Karman, Suite 14
Newport Beach, CA 92660
Tel: (949)250-9060
Fax: (949)250-9063
www.geogroup.net
lrussell@geogroup.net

Advance Praise

"*Winning in FastTime* is an excellent read for anyone thinking through how to escalate organizational change -- not just through strategy development, but through execution. The implementation piece is the one that frequently does not get the attention it deserves. Highly recommended for all managers eager to bring about change."

> —Kathryn Johnson, CEO, The Health Forum

"*Winning in FastTime* synthesizes the lessons of modern hyper war in terms of today's highly competitive corporate culture. Warden and Russell have captured the combat genie and taught it to speak business strategy."

> —General Mike Dugan, USAF (ret.)
> President and CEO of the National Multiple
> Sclerosis Society and former Chief of Staff
> of the United States Air Force

"*Winning in FastTime* translates the Pentagon's strategic process into a timely solution for today's corporate leaders. The Prometheus Principles it presents are based on systematic analysis, parallel change initiatives, and engagement of the entire workforce to achieve strategic targets. *Winning in FastTime* should be required reading for all managers hoping to understand and overtake the market forces of the 21st century."

> —Mary G. Davis
> President of Davis Consulting Group LLC

"Prometheus is the killer app for every leader, manager, business owner—and individual—who wants to win in the digital economy."

> —Gary Esolen, CEO of TravelPlace.com

"Prometheus is the most powerful intellectual capital we have discovered for the rapid creation of breakthrough corporate strategy by clients of all sizes, ranging from the Fortune 100 to the fast-emerging leaders of the New Economy. Because it is a dynamic catalyst of value creation, we expose all of the companies in which we invest to the Prometheus Process."
>   —Walter Schindler, Chairman and CEO
>   Odyssey Strategic Partners

"I've used components of Prometheus for everything from designing video games, writing television bibles to general life planning. While the focus of the book is in business applications, the FastTime philosophy can be used in nearly every area of life or business that needs planning.
>   —Flint Dille, President, Ground Zero
>   Platinum Game Designer, Writer

"Prometheus is not another academic theory. It's a proven, practical system that's helped us win in a fast-moving, difficult-to-predict business environment."
>   —Cliff Tompkins, CEO, Paging Dimensions, Inc.

"John Warden wrote the best book on air strategy and he was the architect of the Air Campaign in the Gulf War. Now he and Leland Russell have given the business world a great gift. A handy guide to strategy, *Winning in FastTime* is packed full of useful ideas that have great practical value for business leaders at all levels. Highly recommended."
>   —Major General Perry M. Smith, USAF (ret.)
>   CNN's military analyst during the Gulf War and
>   author of the best selling book on leadership,
>   *Rules and Tools for Leaders*

"Prometheus transforms planning into action, strategy into results and vision into achievement. It's a powerful tool to organize people to win in the new economy."
                    —John Burke, COO, Hub One Logistics, Inc.

"At first I was skeptical about the relevance of military strategy to business but I was pleasantly surprised. This is a great book on strategy with lots of practical concepts and ideas that will help any organization improve its strategy, and more importantly, its strategic thinking."
                    —James F. Bolt, Chairman
                    Executive Development Associates,
                    author of *Executive Development: A Strategy for Corporate Competitiveness*

"This book presents a systematic, pragmatic approach to conceiving and implementing winning strategies. An important read for executives interested in creating a strategic architecture for the future."
                    —Robert M. Fulmer, Distinguished Visiting
                    Professor of Strategy, Graziadio School of Business
                    and Management, Pepperdine University,
                    co-author, *Leadership By Design* and
                    The Leadership Investment

"We have had the era of the Daniel Bell's and the era of the Peter Drucker's, now is the time for a new business paradigm and John Warden and Leland Russell have just provided it."
                    —Dr. Richard P. Hallion, The Air Force Historian

"In this fast changing environment, the future is impossible to predict and very difficult to react to after the fact. Through the approach described in this book, you become instrumental in creating your future, which allows you to be proactive and much more effective in getting your desired results."

— Wayne B. Bailey, Vice President, Strategy,
The Martin-Brower Company L.L.C.

"*Winning in FastTime* is a must read for leaders who want to thrive in the new economy. This straight-shooting clear-thinking book outlines a powerful approach to thinking strategically and thereby building an enduring and profitable enterprise."

— Bruce Flanz, COO,
Jamaica Hospital Medical Center

"*Winning in FastTime* should be a required handbook for 21st century leaders. It provides a road map that can help make the difference between winning and losing."

— Marshall Goldsmith
Wall Street Journal "Top Ten" leadership development consultant and
co-editor of *The Leader of the Future*

"I had the privilege of being part of John Warden's core team that planned and communicated how to organize the Gulf War for victory quickly. This book shows how the best of modern military strategic thinking that was used with such great success in the Gulf War can be applied directly to business and elsewhere—and why it is essential to do this. This book provides an excellent way for people in non-military settings, where there is a great deal of competition and interactivity, to learn from recent military experience and thought. It is thought provoking and is filled with brilliant insights."

—Terrence R. Colvin, Ph.D.
Chairman, Synergy, Inc.

"*Winning in FastTime* stands out from all the others on strategy. It is cogent and compelling. It puts a complex theory into the hands of the leader or manager so that ideas can be clearly understood and implemented on a small or large scale. A must-read in this changing world."

—Beverly Kaye, President, Career Systems
International, co-author, *Love 'Em or Lose 'Em:
Getting Good People To Stay*

"Warden and Russell ask the right question: How is it possible to plan strategically, let alone win, in an era of warp-speed competition and change? All of us as leaders and as human beings need to learn their answer."

—Nancy J. Adler, Professor of Global Management,
McGill University

"There have been many attempts to apply military strategy to business. Very few are even marginally useful. Now the brilliant planner of the Gulf air war and his co-author have finally succeeded. Utterly original, their method has already been applied with much success. It turns purposeful innovation into the most powerful instrument of success."

—Edward N. Luttwak, Senior Fellow,
Center for Strategic and Studies